PULSE

PULSE

MODERN RECIPES WITH BEANS, PEAS & LENTILS

ELEANOR MAIDMENT

Photography by **Mowie Kay**

RYLAND PETERS & SMALL
LONDON • NEW YORK

For my beautiful
little bean, Maya.

Senior Designer Toni Kay
Senior Editor Abi Waters
Head of Production
  Patricia Harrington
Creative Director
  Leslie Harrington
Editorial Director Julia Charles
Food Stylist Troy Willis
Prop Stylist Hannah Wilkinson

Indexer Vanessa Bird

First published in 2025 by
Ryland Peters & Small
20–21 Jockey's Fields, London
WC1R 4BW
and
1452 Davis Bugg Road
Warrenton, NC 27589

10 9 8 7 6 5 4 3 2 1

Text © Eleanor Maidment 2025
Design and photography
© Ryland Peters & Small 2025

Cover illustration © Adobe Stock/
oleg7799

Printed in China.

ISBN: 978-1-78879-675-0

A CIP record for this book is
available from the British Library.
US Library of Congress cataloging-
in-Publication Data has been
applied for.

NOTES
· All spoon measurements are level
unless otherwise specified.

· All eggs are medium (UK) or large
(US), unless specified as large, in
which case US extra-large should be
used. Uncooked or partially cooked
eggs should not be served to the
very old, frail, young children,
pregnant women or those with
compromised immune systems.

· When a recipe calls for cling film/
plastic wrap, you can substitute for
beeswax wraps, silicone stretch lids
or compostable baking paper for
greater sustainability.

· When a recipe calls for the grated
zest of citrus fruit, buy unwaxed
fruit and wash well before using.

· Ovens should be preheated to
the specified temperatures.

MIX
Paper | Supporting
responsible forestry
FSC® C008047

CONTENTS

INTRODUCTION

I have loved writing this book. It has been a wonderfully creative exploration of how easy and enjoyable it is to cook with pulses. The truth is that I have not always been a huge fan of dried beans, lentils and chickpeas. I wasn't convinced by their texture, found them a bit bland and never had time to faff about soaking and boiling them. But over the last couple of years I slowly started to include many more pulses in my recipes, both in my capacity as a home cook and as a food writer. And I was starting to really enjoy them. So why the marked change?

BETTER QUALITY

Pulses have been eaten by people throughout history and today form part of the staple diet in many countries. Not in the UK. Our most eaten pulse is the haricot/navy bean and that's because we consume them as baked beans (and those beans are imported from the States, anyway!). Traditionally pulses were considered food of the poor and so we have invested very little in their farming. Finally the tides are turning and higher quality pulses are more widely available. British brands like Bold Bean Co. and Hodmedod's are committed to bringing us more varieties of legumes and you can absolutely taste the difference. They're plump, creamy and flavourful. As well as these homegrown options, we also have greater access to imported pulses from countries likes Spain where they are supported agriculturally and highly prized.

GREAT VALUE

It is hardly coincidence that I started cooking more with pulses just as we went through one of the worst cost of living crises in decades. In the early 2020s food inflation was at an all-time high and everyone needed to cut shopping bills. Pulses are fantastic value. Whether dried or ready-cooked, they are a brilliant low-cost way to include protein and fibre in a diet. Even the newer premium brands mentioned above, which do come at a higher price, are still good value if you consider them as an alternative to meat.

GOOD HEALTH

We are much more conscientious about what we eat nowadays. It is clear that what we put inside our bodies has long-term implications and there is much science-backed evidence on the health benefits of pulses. They are a good source of plant-based protein, they provide fibre, which is essential for a healthy gut, they count towards our five a day and are packed with vitamins, minerals and antioxidants.

ENVIRONMENTAL BENEFITS

For the sake of our planet we need to adapt our diets to include more plant-based proteins... and with some urgency. Intensive animal farming is driving deforestation, creating greenhouse gases and polluting our water systems. Meanwhile the ecological arguments for farming more pulses are indisputable: they're sustainable, easy to grow, water efficient and actually have positive implications for the environment. Many plants in the legume family are 'nitrogen fixers' meaning they have the ability to convert nitrogen in the atmosphere into a form that can be used in the soil, making it more fertile for other crops.

These were all very convincing incentives to eat more pulses and, as I started to cook with them more, I also realized just how underrated they are. They are easy to prepare, so versatile in the ways they can be cooked and there are very few ingredients they don't go with. I hope this book demonstrates how rewarding and wholesome it is to eat pulses every day, without sacrificing the foods you already love. We should all be eating more pulses, and now is a good time to start!

A WHISTLE-STOP GUIDE TO PULSES

Firstly it is important to clarify what exactly is meant by 'pulses'. They are the dried (as opposed to fresh) edible seeds that are found in the pods of plants in the legume family, and this includes all dried beans, peas and lentils. There are many varieties and you'll find that different countries around the world cultivate their favoured species.

I have tried to stick to the most commonly available pulses and have listed them out here. As our appetites for pulses grow I expect we will see more and more varieties on offer, and I urge you to experiment with new and different options where you can.

Aduki beans – a small mahogany coloured bean that is popular in East Asian cooking. They are used in savoury dishes, and also to make red bean paste which is often used in sweets.

Beluga lentils – delicate, glossy black lentils that are said to resemble beluga caviar. They hold their shape well when cooked and look gorgeous in salads.

Black beans – also known as black turtle beans and popular in Latin American cooking, these beans are great in chillies, salsas and salads. Their rich, purple-black colour means they're a good source of polyphenols.

Black eyed beans/peas – distinctive with their black spots on an otherwise off-white bean, these are popular in southern US cuisine and in parts of Africa. They're lovely and creamy when cooked.

Borlotti/cranberry beans – uncooked borlottis are a beauty of a bean with their mottled cream and cranberry-red skins. Once cooked they turn a russet colour with a soft texture. Popular in Italian cooking.

Brown lentils – a great-value lentil (which are so called because of their 'lens'-like shape), with a mild flavour and soft texture.

Butter/lima beans – these large, plump beans have sky-rocketed in popularity in recent years. They're a popular choice when swapping meat out of recipes as they feel substantial and meaty.

Cannellini beans – one of the most widely available white beans, these are mild and creamy and a good all-purpose option.

Carlin peas – expect to hear more about these small, nutty brown peas. They are becoming more widely available in shops, both dried and pre-cooked, and make a great alternative to chickpeas with a similarly impressive nutrient profile.

Chickpeas/garbanzo beans – are actually a type of bean. They have a distinctively nutty flavour and can be eaten whole, crushed or blended until smooth (most commonly in houmous). If anyone tells me they don't like chickpeas, I tell them to buy a jar of Bold Bean Co's queen chickpeas. They're a large variety which is exceptionally plump and tasty!

Flageolet beans – these are immature haricot beans, small in size and light green colour. Probably France's most popular bean.

French green lentils – very small lentils that are mottled slate-grey and dark green. They are firm when cooked with slightly peppery notes.

Haricot/navy beans – the original baked bean, haricots are a small and very tender white bean that can be used interchangeably with cannellini.

Kidney beans – eaten most commonly in the UK in chilli con carne, these deep red beans are so called because of their shape. As with black and aduki beans, their deep colours means they are high in polyphenols.

Mung beans & moong dal - neither classified as a bean or as a lentil, mung beans are small, green pulses (also known as green gram). Popular in Asian cooking, they tend to be sold dried and should be sufficiently soaked before cooking until they start to soften and split. When mung beans are split open and dried, they become yellow moong dal. When whole mung beans are sprouted, they become beansprouts.

Pinto beans – popular in Mexican and Tex-Mex cooking, smooth and earthy pintos are commonly used to make refried beans.

Puy/French lentils – often consider the king of lentils, puy lentils must be grown in a designated area of France. They are robust, nutty and wonderful in salads.

Red split lentils – these cook very quickly from dried and break down into a pulpy texture making them popular in soups and stews.

Split yellow peas – popular in British cooking, split yellow peas were traditionally used in pease pudding and split pea soup. They can be cooked relatively quickly from dried to become soft, mellow and wonderfully comforting.

COOKING WITH PULSES

DRIED, CANNED OR JARRED?
Whether you choose dried pulses or those that have been pre-cooked is totally up to you. Personally I couldn't live without the convenience of cans and jars, and I have written these recipes assuming that many people will choose canned as they are quick to cook, readily available and great value. If you prefer to cook pulses from dried then by all means do so, they are wonderful this way and you can add aromatics (such as onions, bay leaves and black peppercorns) as they simmer.

If cooking from dried, expect pulses to roughly double in weight after cooking. I would also advise to always follow the pack instructions as soaking and cooking times can vary between species. And always make sure that they are cooked until completely soft; under-cooked beans are neither pleasant nor easy to digest, I warn you! In the case of kidney beans, they can be toxic if undercooked, so always be extra vigilant that they have been boiled for a minimum of 10 minutes.

CHOOSING THE BEST QUALITY
In any major supermarket you should find a good variety of pulses, not just whether they are dried or pre-cooked, but also different brands, from different origins and at various price points.

It's great to have so much choice, but as with any other ingredient the quality does vary. In the writing of this book, I tasted many different brands of pulses, and some are softer, more tender and more flavoursome than others. I think once you find an option you like and that suits your budget, stick to it. I mentioned in my introduction that Bold Bean Co. do fantastic jarred beans. Personally I think they are worth spending a little extra on, but these recipes have been written so that any pulse can be used.

WHAT IS AQUAFABA?
Dried pulses need to be cooked in water, and at the end of cooking the water becomes a viscous liquid known as aquafaba. Most canned and jarred pre-cooked pulses are stored in this aquafaba and many cooks like to use it as an ingredient. In this book I tend to suggest draining and rinsing most pulses before using. This is because many canned pulses (particularly lower-cost options) contain preserving and firming agents in the water. If you want to use the aquafaba in cooking, then check the ingredients. If it just states the pulse and water then it's fine to use; it has a creamy texture that can add body to sauces and stews. If salt is listed as an ingredient, then have a taste as some can be quite heavily salted. Alternatively, if you are cooking beans from dried you can save some of the cooking water to use in finished dishes too (always discard the soaking water, though).

While on the subject of adding aquafaba or not, consistency is an important thing to consider in many of the recipes in this book. It is often hard to convey exactly how much liquid is needed in soups, stews and sauces. If your instinct tells you a sauce is too loose and the flavour not concentrated enough, simmer it for a little longer. Equally, if it feels too thick, add a splash more water or aquafaba.

THE SECRET TO CRISPY PULSES
Crispy chickpeas/garbanzo beans and crispy beans (usually butter/lima or cannellini) make a great snack. Having made them on many occasions, using various methods, I feel it is my duty to let you know that the

key to their success is making sure they're well dried before you cook them. Ideally rinse, then pat dry on a clean kitchen towel and leave to air dry for as long as you can before cooking with oil. Air fryers are probably the best and most efficient cooking method. A conventional oven will take a bit longer, and I also find pan-frying chickpeas works well. If you're adding spices, I would toss with the pulses towards the end of cooking (for the last few minutes) to avoid them burning.

LAYER UP SEASONING

In general pulses are quite mild in flavour, which is great because they can happily be paired with strong and punchy ingredients. It also means you need to be judicious with seasoning to help them shine. In many recipes I have given a quantity of salt to include, but I would still suggest tasting at the end to check the seasoning. When salt is not listed in quantity, I advise layering it as you cook to help coax out the flavour of other ingredients. As well as using classic seasonings of salt and pepper, I often find that a squeeze of lemon juice (or another acid) can really help to bring depth. Together salt and acid are very effective flavour enhancers.

AND FINALLY...

In my recipe writing I always aim to be as precise and descriptive as possible with ingredients, methods and equipment, but remember that every kitchen differs, produce varies and every cook has slightly different tastes. Trust your instinct when cooking, if you think something needs a little more time or a little less of an ingredient, then go with it. You are always your best guide.

EASY
WEEKNIGHTS

It would be perfectly possible to write an entire book entitled 'beans on toast'. It is a supper that we already love (with baked beans of course) and the variations are endless. This is one of my favourites.

PANCETTA, LEEKS & BEANS ON TOAST

1¹/₂ tbsp olive oil
75 g/2³/₄ oz. diced smoked
   pancetta
2 leeks, trimmed, halved
   lengthways and thinly sliced
1 rosemary sprig, leaves finely
   chopped
1 x 400-g/14-oz can haricot/
   navy beans, drained and
   rinsed
100 ml/scant ¹/₂ cup chicken
   stock (or liquid from the can
   of beans if using)
2 tbsp crème fraîche
2 eggs
2 slices sourdough
salt and black pepper
grated Parmesan or pecorino,
   to serve

SERVES 2

Heat ¹/₂ tablespoon oil in a large frying pan/skillet over a medium-high heat. Fry the pancetta for 4–5 minutes until starting to colour a little. Add the leeks and fry for 4–5 minutes until softened.

Stir in the rosemary and beans, then add the stock and bubble gently until most of the liquid has evaporated. Stir the crème fraîche into the leeks and beans and cook for a final couple of minutes, then take off the heat and season to taste.

Meanwhile, heat the remaining 1 tablespoon oil in a small frying pan over a medium-high heat and fry the eggs, basting the yolks with some of the oil to help them cook evenly.

Toast the sourdough and place on plates. Spoon over the leeks and beans and grate over a little Parmesan. Top each with a fried egg, season the tops with salt and pepper and grate over a little more cheese to serve.

COOK'S TIP *For a vegetarian version use chopped sundried tomatoes instead of pancetta and fry for just a couple of minutes before adding the leeks. Use a vegetarian hard cheese instead of the Parmesan.*

PULSE SWAP *This is a great recipe for experimenting with different varieties of beans. Try borlotti/cranberry, butter/lima, cannellini or flageolet beans.*

This is loosely based on a classic stroganoff: rich, warming and a perfect weeknight supper. Adding the beans means you need less meat; a great way of saving money and adding a sustainable, plant-based protein.

SMOKY, CREAMY BUTTER BEANS, MUSHROOMS & STEAK

2 x 200-g/7-oz. sirloin steaks
1 tbsp olive oil
250 g/9 oz. chestnut/cremini mushrooms, thickly sliced
1 large onion, halved and thinly sliced
1 scant tsp sweet smoked paprika
1 x 400-g/14-oz. can butter/lima beans, drained and rinsed
200 ml/scant 1 cup fresh chicken (or beef) stock
1 1/2 tsp Worcestershire sauce
3 tbsp soured cream
handful of flat-leaf parsley, roughly chopped
salt and black pepper
rice, tagliatelle or a green salad, to serve

SERVES 4

Take the steaks out of the fridge at least 30 minutes before cooking. Remove from the packaging, season and set aside until ready to cook.

Heat the oil in a large frying pan/skillet over a high heat. When smoking hot, fry the steaks for 2 minutes on each side. Remove from the pan and set aside to rest.

Lower the heat under the pan to medium-high and add the mushrooms and onion with a pinch of salt. Fry for 10 minutes, stirring regularly, until starting to turn golden in places.

Add the paprika and a good grind of black pepper and fry for a minute more, then add the beans, stock and Worcestershire sauce. Simmer for 5 minutes, then stir in the soured cream.

Slice the steak and add to the pan along with any carving juices. Scatter with parsley and serve with rice or tagliatelle, or just enjoy as it is with a green salad.

COOK'S TIP *If the steaks have a thick strip of fat on them and you wish to eat it, hold them with tongs and cook on the fat side for a minute or so to crisp up before removing from the pan. If you prefer not to eat the fat, then cut it off when carving (but leave on during cooking as it will release flavour into the pan).*

PULSE SWAP *Any white beans will work here. Try cannellini or haricot/navy, or even borlotti/cranberry.*

This is a mild and mellow curry that can be on the table in about 30 minutes and is a really good option for kids (minus the red chilli/chile).

TURMERIC & COCONUT CHICKEN with chickpeas

1 tbsp neutral oil (e.g. sunflower or vegetable)
4 chicken thigh fillets (about 350 g/ 12½ oz. in total)
1 onion, halved and thinly sliced
1½ tsp finely grated fresh root ginger
½ tsp ground turmeric
2 tsp mild curry powder
1 x 400-g/14 oz. can chickpeas/garbanzo beans, drained and rinsed
1 x 400-g/14-oz. can coconut milk
juice of ½ lime
100 g/2 cups spinach
sliced red chilli/chile, coriander/cilantro leaves and steamed rice, to serve
salt and black pepper

SERVES 4

Heat the oil in a large frying or sauté pan/skillet, or a shallow casserole over a medium-high heat. Cut the chicken into 2.5-cm/1-inch pieces and season with salt. Add to the pan with the onion and fry, stirring regularly, for 8–10 minutes until just turning golden in places.

Add the ginger, turmeric, curry powder, a good grind of black pepper and another pinch of salt and fry over the heat for another 2 minutes. Stir in the chickpeas, then the coconut milk. Bring to a gentle simmer and cook for 10 minutes, stirring occasionally. The chicken should be cooked by now.

Squeeze in the lime juice and check the seasoning; you may need a little more salt or lime juice. Stir in the spinach leaves and allow to wilt in the pan for a couple of minutes. Sprinkle over some sliced chilli and coriander, and serve with steamed rice

COOK'S TIP *You can easily double up this recipe to serve a crowd; any leftovers will freeze well. You can also make it a day in advance, adding the spinach when reheating to serve.*

PULSE SWAP *Black beans or butter/lima beans.*

SUPER GREEN BAKED BEANS

2 tbsp olive oil
1 leek, trimmed and sliced
2 garlic cloves, crushed
200 g/7 oz. Swiss chard, stalks chopped and leaves shredded
200 g/4 cups fresh spinach
150 g/5½ oz. ricotta
zest of ½ unwaxed lemon
30 g/⅓ cup grated Parmesan
1 x 400-g/14-oz. can butter/lima beans, drained and rinsed
handful of basil leaves, shredded
salt and black pepper

SERVES 2–3

Preheat the oven to 200°C/180°C fan/400°F/ Gas 6. Heat the oil in large ovenproof frying pan/ skillet over a medium-high heat. Fry the leek, garlic and chard stalks with a pinch of salt, stirring regularly, for 5 minutes. Add the spinach and the shredded chard leaves to the pan and cook, stirring regularly, for 3–4 minutes until the leaves are wilted.

Meanwhile, in a bowl, mix the ricotta, lemon zest and two-thirds of the Parmesan with some salt and a good grind of pepper. Take the pan off the heat and stir the ricotta through the greens, then stir through the beans and basil. (At this stage you can leave the dish for up to an hour before finishing in the oven.) Scatter the remaining Parmesan over the top. Bake for 10 minutes before serving.

COOK'S TIP *I love the earthiness of chard, but you could use any greens in this dish. Cavolo nero is great or spring greens are an economical option.*

PULSE SWAP *You could use any beans here – try cannellini or kidney – or chickpeas/garbanzo beans work well, too.*

Pictured on page 20

A glorious tangle of leafy greens, zesty ricotta and bulbous beans. This is a handy dish that you can prepare in advance and then pop in the oven to heat up before serving with crusty bread or as a side dish to roast chicken or fish.

Chorizo, chickpeas and white fish are very happy bedfellows. This is an elegant supper for two that would happily be washed down with a crisp glass of white.

SEA BASS, CHICKPEAS & CHORIZO

2 tbsp olive oil
1 large courgette/zucchini, cut into 2-cm/³/₄-inch cubes
1 garlic clove, finely chopped
80 g/3 oz. cooking chorizo, cut into small chunks
1 x 400-g/14-oz. can chickpeas/ garbanzo beans, drained and rinsed
100 ml/scant ¹/₂ cup chicken or vegetable stock
juice of ¹/₂ lemon
2 sea bass (see cook's tip)
1 tbsp chopped dill or parsley
salt and black pepper
lemon wedges, to serve

SERVES 2

Heat 1 tablespoon of the oil in a large frying pan/skillet over a medium-high heat. Fry the courgette with a pinch of salt for 3 minutes, then add the garlic and cook for another 3 minutes, stirring occasionally. Add the chorizo to the pan and fry, stirring regularly, for another 5 minutes.

Add the chickpeas and fry for a couple of minutes coating them in the oil, then add the stock and bubble until reduced by about half. Take off the heat and squeeze over a little lemon juice.

In another large frying pan, heat the remaining 1 tablespoon of oil over a high heat. Pat the sea bass fillets dry on paper towels. Slash the skin side three times and season all over. Fry skin-side down for 3 minutes, pressing them lightly with a spatula to flatten. Carefully turn the fillets, then take the pan off the heat. Squeeze a little more lemon juice into the pan (not directly onto the fish) and leave them to cook in the residual heat for a minute.

Spoon the chickpeas, chorizo and courgette onto plates and top with the sea bass. Sprinkle with chopped herbs and serve immediately with lemon wedges.

COOK'S TIP *Any white fish would be happy in this dish. You could simply substitute sea bream or red mullet fillets, or try a chunky piece of cod or hake, increasing the cooking time accordingly.*

PULSE SWAP *Butter/lima beans would also work well in this recipe.*

This makes a brilliant midweek supper for two. You can prepare the squash sauce up to 48 hours in advance, then just reheat it in the pan before adding the pasta and the beans. You can also make double the sauce and freeze half to use at a later date.

SQUASH, SAGE & WHITE BEAN PASTA

2 tbsp olive oil
200 g/7 oz. peeled and deseeded butternut squash, cut into 1-cm/½-inch dice
1 onion, finely diced
½ tsp salt
8 sage leaves, finely sliced
1 garlic clove, finely chopped
150 ml/⅔ cup chicken or vegetable stock
1 x 400-g/14-oz. can cannellini beans, drained and rinsed
150 g/5½ oz. penne or other pasta shape
2 tbsp single/light cream
20 g/¼ cup finely grated pecorino or Parmesan, plus extra to serve
salt and black pepper
crispy sage leaves, to serve (optional; see cook's tip)

SERVES 2

Heat the oil in a large frying pan/skillet over a medium-high heat. Fry the squash, onion and salt for 10 minutes until just starting to turn golden. Add the sage and garlic and fry, stirring, for another 6–7 minutes until everything is soft and golden.

Add the stock and one-third (80 g/generous ⅓ cup) of the beans, simmering until the liquid has reduced by half. By now the squash should be completely soft, if not add a splash more water and continue to cook until you can easily mash it with a fork.

Meanwhile, bring a large saucepan of salted water to the boil. Add the pasta and cook for a minute less than the pack instructions.

Take the pan of squash off the heat, stir in the cream and tip everything into a small high-speed blender (a Nutribullet works well). Add the grated cheese and a good grind of black pepper and whizz until smooth. Check the seasoning.

Scoop out a cupful of the pasta cooking water, then drain the pasta. Tip the pasta back into the saucepan with the remaining beans and the squash sauce. Stir over a medium heat for 1 minute, adding a splash of the pasta cooking water to loosen if needed. Divide between shallow bowls and serve with extra grated cheese and crispy sage leaves, if liked.

COOK'S TIP *This is great with crispy sage leaves on top. Heat 2 tablespoons oil in a small frying pan and add 3–4 sage leaves per person. Fry for 1–2 minutes on each side or until dark green and crisp. Pat dry on a paper towel before scattering over the pasta.*

PULSE SWAP *Try haricot/navy, butter/lima or flageolet beans instead of cannellini.*

This recipe appears to have a lot of ingredients, but many are repeated and it is extremely simple to put together. Plus the finished dish is the best sandwich you will ever eat. I advise investing in good flatbreads; it will make a difference.

AUBERGINE, EGG & CHICKPEA FLATBREADS with tahini dressing

ROASTED AUBERGINE
2 aubergines/
  eggplants, trimmed
  and cut into 2-cm/
  ³/4-inch thick rounds
3 tbsp olive oil
2 tbsp honey
2 tbsp lemon juice
salt

CRISPY CHICKPEAS
1/2 x 400-g/14-oz.
  can chickpeas/
  garbanzo beans,
  drained and rinsed
1 tbsp olive oil
heaped 1/4 tsp ground
  cumin
zest of 1/2 lemon

**QUICK HOUMOUS
  (or use 150 g/5¹/2 oz.
  shop-bought)**
1/2 x 400-g/14-oz. can
  chickpeas, drained
  and rinsed
3–4 tbsp warm water

3 tbsp tahini
2 tbsp lemon juice
1 tbsp olive oil
1 small garlic clove
1/4 tsp salt
pinch of paprika and
  ground cumin

TAHINI DRESSING
2 tbsp tahini
2–3 tbsp cold water
1 tbsp lemon juice

TO SERVE
2 flatbreads or 4 pitta
  breads
3 hard-boiled eggs,
  sliced
2 tomatoes, diced
1/4 red onion, sliced
chopped flat-leaf
  parsley

MAKES 2 LARGE
OR 4 SMALL
SANDWICHES

Preheat the oven to 220°C/200°C fan/425°F/Gas 7. Brush the aubergine slices on each side with oil and season with salt. Spread over a large parchment-lined baking tray and roast for 10 minutes. Mix the honey and lemon juice. Brush over both sides of the aubergine, then return to the oven for 20 minutes, turning halfway. Meanwhile, make the crispy chickpeas, houmous and tahini dressing.

For the crispy chickpeas, toss all the ingredients together with a good pinch of salt. Add to a small frying pan/skillet and cook over a high heat for about 10 minutes, tossing regularly.

For the houmous, place all the ingredients in a small high-speed blender and whizz until smooth. Check the seasoning and add more water as needed.

For the tahini dressing, whisk all the ingredients together in a small bowl with a pinch of salt. Aim for a consistency of double/heavy cream, adding more water if needed.

To assemble, heat the flatbreads or pitta according to pack instructions, or for a couple of minutes in the oven. Spread generously with houmous, then pile on the aubergine, sliced eggs, tomatoes, onion and parsley. Drizzle with the tahini dressing and scatter with the crispy chickpeas.

Puy lentils were the first pulse I truly fell in love with; they are nutty and firm and have a sophisticated air about them. This is a salad full of flavours that are just meant to be together. I think it tastes best when you roast the beetroot from scratch, although a ready-cooked option will make this recipe much quicker and will still taste superb.

HOT SMOKED SALMON, BEETROOT & LENTIL SALAD with horseradish dressing

300 g/10½ oz. raw beetroot/ beets (or 330 g/12 oz. ready-cooked beetroot)
3 tbsp olive oil
1 tbsp red or white wine vinegar
1 tsp Dijon mustard
1 tsp runny honey
½ tsp salt
250 g/9 oz. cooked Puy lentils
2 spring onions/scallions, thinly sliced
40 g/1½ oz. watercress, in small bunches
180 g/6 oz. hot smoked salmon, flaked

HORSERADISH DRESSING
3 tbsp Greek-style natural/ plain yogurt
1 tbsp hot horseradish sauce
1 tbsp chopped dill
salt and black pepper

SERVES 2

Preheat the oven to 200°C/180°C fan/400°F/Gas 6.

Trim and peel the beetroot and then cut into slim wedges. Toss with 1 tablespoon oil, season and spread over a baking tray. Roast for 30–40 minutes, turning every 15 minutes, until tender and a little caramelized.

In a mixing bowl, whisk together the remaining 2 tablespoons oil with the vinegar, mustard, honey and salt. While they're still hot, add the roasted beetroot to the vinaigrette and toss together; set aside to cool. (If using ready cooked beetroot, just add to the dressing at room temperature.)

In a bowl, mix all the ingredients for the horseradish dressing with salt and pepper.

When the beetroot are at room temperature, toss with the lentils spring onions, watercress and flaked fish. Divide between plates and serve with the horseradish dressing.

COOK'S TIP *Smoked mackerel or hot-smoked trout also work really well in this salad. Vegetarians could add some goat's cheese instead of fish if preferred.*

PULSE SWAP *Any cooked black, green or brown lentil will do here, ideally a firmer variety.*

This beautifully simple recipe was suggested to me by a Catalan friend, who makes it with highly prized Santa Pao beans. This is my version, and I would suggest seeking out a jar of good-quality Spanish white beans to make it. A brilliant cold-weather supper.

CATALAN-STYLE WHITE BEANS & SAUSAGES

4 tbsp olive oil
8 pork sausages (I often buy
   ones with fennels seeds)
4 large garlic cloves, thinly sliced
700-g/1¹/₂-lb. jar Spanish white
   beans and their liquid
   (see cook's tip)
squeeze of lemon juice (optional)
large handful of chopped
   flat-leaf parsley
salt and black pepper
wilted or steamed greens,
   to serve

SERVES 4

Preheat the oven to 180°C/160°C fan/350°F/Gas 4.

Heat 2 tablespoons oil in a large frying pan/skillet over a medium-high heat. Add the sausages and fry, turning regularly, for 10 minutes until brown all over. Transfer to a roasting tin and place in the oven for 5–10 minutes, or until cooked through.

Meanwhile, add the remaining 2 tablespoons oil to the pan and lower the heat to medium. Add the garlic and fry for 1–2 minutes until golden and fragrant. Add the jar of beans and their liquid and stir together. Cook gently over the heat for 3–4 minutes.

Taste the beans, and add salt, pepper and a squeeze of lemon juice if it needs it. Stir through the parsley and serve the beans with the sausages. Some wilted greens go nicely alongside.

COOK'S TIP *Perella alagarda beans or Brindisa Navarrico haricot/ navy are both good options. The bean liquid often contains salt (and sausages are often quite salty too), so always taste before you add extra salt.*

PULSE SWAP *If you can't get hold of a jar of Spanish beans, use cannellini or haricot/navy. If using canned, check the bean liquid doesn't contain anything unusual before using. Alternatively, you can add 100–150 ml/scant ½–⅔ cup water or stock with the beans, or the bean cooking liquid if you have cooked them from dried.*

This is the kind of dish I feel like could be on a gastropub menu and it's something I often make on a Friday night. My local independent shop gets its fish delivery on a Friday and usually there's chalk stream trout. It's a sustainable alternative to salmon, which is sadly over-farmed in this country. Of course, salmon would be fine here too though.

TROUT, CURRIED LEEKS & BEANS

35 g/2 tbsp unsalted butter
1 tsp nigella/black onion seeds
2 leeks (about 350 g/12¹/₂ oz.), trimmed, halved lengthways and sliced
1 scant tsp curry powder
1 x 400-g/14-oz. can cannellini beans, drained (reserving liquid, see below) and rinsed
100–150 ml/scant ¹/₂–²/₃ cup bean liquid (or use chicken or veg stock)
4 tbsp single/light cream
1 tbsp olive oil
2 x 120-g/4-oz. fillets chalk stream trout (or salmon)
a squeeze of lemon juice
mango chutney (I like Geeta's), to serve

SERVES 4

Heat 25 g/1¹/₂ tablespoons butter in a large frying pan/skillet over a medium heat. Add the nigella seeds and cook for a minute, then add the leeks and a good pinch of salt and sweat gently for 8–10 minutes. They should be bright and green, but also soft and sweet.

Add the curry powder and fry for a couple more minutes, then stir in the beans and their liquid (or stock). Bring to the simmer and cook for 2–3 minutes, then stir in the cream and simmer for a minute more; set aside off the heat.

In a small frying pan, heat the oil over a medium-high heat. Pat the fish dry on a paper towel, then season lightly all over. Place skin-side down in the pan and fry for 3 minutes. Turn the fish, lowering the heat to medium and cook for another 2 minutes, then add the remaining 10 g/¹/₂ tablespoon butter to the pan and a squeeze of lemon and cook for a final 1 minute.

Reheat the leeks and beans if necessary, then divide among plates. Place the trout fillets on top and spoon over some mango chutney. Serve immediately.

COOK'S TIP *You can make the beans and leeks up to 48 hours in advance, then reheat to serve, adding a splash of water to loosen if needed.*

PULSE SWAP *Any white beans would be great in this recipe, try butter/lima or haricot/navy.*

I am well aware that the canned black (turtle) beans we buy are different to the fermented black soybeans that are used in Asian cooking, but this recipe works really well and the beans turn into a glossy sauce that coats the noodles.

SPRING ONION & BLACK BEAN NOODLES with chilli oil

2 bunches spring onions/
  scallions (about 200 g/7 oz.),
  trimmed
100 ml/scant 1/2 cup vegetable oil
1 x 400-g/14-oz. can black
  beans, drained and rinsed
3 nests of dried medium egg
  noodles
3–4 tbsp dark soy sauce
1 tbsp Japanese rice vinegar
  (or balsamic vinegar
  works too)
1 1/2–2 tsp caster/superfine sugar
1 tsp toasted sesame oil
toasted sesame seeds and
  crispy chilli/chile oil, to garnish
  (optional)

SERVES 3

Cut the spring onions into 5-cm/2-inch pieces, then cut each piece lengthways into strips. (This is the best way to cut them but if you're short on time just roughly chop them into 1–2-cm/1/2–3/4-inch chunks.)

Heat the oil in a saucepan over a medium heat. Set aside a small amount of the spring onions to garnish, then add the rest to the oil with a small pinch of salt. Fry, stirring often, for 5 minutes. Add the beans and cook for another 15–20 minutes, stirring occasionally, until the onions are golden and fragrant and the beans are soft and broken down.

Just before the beans and onions are ready, prepare the noodles according to the pack instructions.

To the beans add 3 tablespoons of the soy sauce, the vinegar, 1 1/2 teaspoons of the sugar and the sesame oil and stir together. Taste and see if you need to add more soy or sugar. Take off the heat and stir in the warm noodles.

Divide among shallow bowls and garnish with the reserved spring onions, some toasted sesame seeds and crispy chilli oil, if you like.

COOK'S TIP *These noodles are great as they are, but you could happily toss in some cooked king prawns/jumbo shrimp and broccoli florets or shredded sugar snaps along with the noodles to bulk the recipe up.*

PULSE SWAP *Aduki beans would also work well here.*

Carlin peas are a British pulse that we are likely to be seeing a lot more of as our appetites for legumes grow. They're brown and nutty with a lovely creamy texture and make a great alternative to chickpeas. You can absolutely replace them with chickpeas in this recipe.

CARLIN PEA, QUINOA & HALLOUMI SALAD

100 g/generous ¹/₂ cup dried quinoa or 250 g/generous 1 cup cooked quinoa

240 g/1¹/₂ cups cooked carlin peas (or chickpeas/garbanzo beans), drained and rinsed

2 tbsp olive oil, plus a little extra for brushing

200 g/7 oz. Tenderstem broccoli, trimmed and cut into 4-cm/1¹/₂-inch lengths

handful of mint leaves, shredded

2 tbsp thinly sliced spring onions/scallions

250-g/9-oz. block halloumi cheese, cut into 1-cm/¹/₂-inch thick slices

salt and black pepper

LIME & CHILLI DRESSING

2 tbsp olive oil

1¹/₂ tbsp lime juice

1 mild red chilli/chile, deseeded and finely chopped

1 tsp runny honey

SERVES 2

Preheat the oven to 200°C/180°C fan/400°F/Gas 6.

If cooking the quinoa from dried, add to a pan of boiling salted water and simmer for 15–17 minutes until tender, then drain.

Toss the cooked quinoa and carlin peas with 1 tablespoon of the oil and a good pinch of salt and spread over a large roasting tray. Roast in the preheated oven for 10 minutes.

Stir up the quinoa and carlin peas. Toss the broccoli with another 1 tablespoon of the oil, season and scatter over the top and return to the oven for 10–12 minutes until the broccoli is tender. Leave to cool for 5 minutes.

Meanwhile, make the dressing by stirring all the ingredients together with a pinch of salt and a grind of black pepper.

Toss the quinoa with the mint and spring onions and arrange over a platter or divide between plates.

Heat a large frying pan/skillet over a medium heat. Brush the halloumi slices with a little oil and fry for 1–2 minutes on each side. Arrange over the salad, drizzle over the dressing and serve.

COOK'S TIP *There are lots of great ways to cook halloumi – under the grill/broiler, in an air-fryer, on a griddle pan or barbecue, choose whichever one you prefer.*

LIGHT & SUMMERY

This sings of Mediterranean summers. You can happily save yourself 20 minutes by using roasted peppers from a jar, although it does taste best when you take the time to grill them yourself.

SEARED TUNA, WHITE BEANS & ROASTED PEPPERS

2 red (bell) peppers, halved and deseeded
4 tbsp olive oil
1 echalion/banana shallot, halved and thinly sliced lengthways
2 tbsp small capers, such as nonpareille
2 tbsp sultanas/golden raisins or raisins, soaked in warm water
1 tbsp sherry vinegar
1 x 400-g/14-oz. can butter/lima beans, drained and rinsed
large handful of flat-leaf parsley, roughly chopped
2 x 120-g/4-oz. fresh tuna steaks
salt and black pepper

SERVES 2

Preheat the grill/broiler to high. Place the peppers, cut-side down on a foil-lined roasting tray. Grill for 10–12 minutes or until blackened, then place in a bowl and cover the top with a plate; set aside for at least 15 minutes.

Peel the peppers, discarding the skins. Slice the peppers into strips, and return to the bowl keeping any juices that have collected.

Heat 3 tablespoons of the oil in a frying pan/skillet over a medium heat. Fry the shallot and a pinch of salt for 2–3 minutes until soft, then add the capers and fry for a minute more. Drain and roughly chop the sultanas and add to the pan along with the vinegar. Finally, add the peppers and their juices and the butter beans. Stir over the heat for a minute. Add the parsley and set aside.

In a small frying pan, heat the remaining 1 tablespoon oil over a high heat. Season the tuna steaks on both sides and fry. Depending on their thickness and how pink you like it, they'll take around 1–2 minutes on each side. Serve immediately with the peppers and beans.

COOK'S TIP *Any fish would work well in this recipe. Cod or hake fillets or seared salmon would make a good alternative to tuna.*

PULSE SWAP *Haricot/navy, cannellini or flageolet beans would all work well in this recipe.*

This is one of the easiest recipes in the book and makes a great introduction to beans. It can be eaten straight from the roasting tin piled on to toast for a fabulous lunch or can be served as a summery side to roast chicken, grilled fish or lamb chops.

STICKY COURGETTES, TOMATOES & BEANS

500 g/1 lb. 2 oz. courgettes/
    zucchini (about 2 large),
    trimmed and thickly sliced
2 tbsp olive oil, plus extra
    to serve
350 g/12¹/₂ oz. cherry tomatoes,
    halved
3 garlic cloves, sliced
1 x 400-g/14-oz. can cannellini
    beans, drained and rinsed
salt and black pepper
handful of basil leaves,
    to garnish
finely grated Parmesan
    or pecorino, to serve (optional)
toast, to serve (optional)

SERVES 2–4

Preheat the oven to 220°C/200°C fan/440°F/Gas 7.

Toss the courgettes and oil in a large mixing bowl, then scatter into a large roasting tin and season with salt. Roast for 20 minutes.

In the same mixing bowl, add the tomatoes and sliced garlic, tossing them in the residual oil. Scatter into the roasting tin and stir up with the courgettes. Return to the oven for 10 minutes.

Stir in the cannellini beans and season everything with salt and pepper. Roast for another 10–15 minutes until everything is golden and turning caramelized.

Stand out of the oven for 10 minutes, then drizzle with a little more oil, scatter with basil and grate over some Parmesan or pecorino, if you like. Serve on toast or as a side.

COOK'S TIP *You could throw a couple of baking potatoes into the oven while the vegetables are roasting and serve this on top as a simple supper.*

PULSE SWAP *Any white beans would work well in this – try butter/lima beans or haricot/navy. Borlotti/cranberry beans would also be nice.*

Tostadas are crispy, flat tortillas, although you could serve these simply as tacos. The avocado and chicken topping is inspired by a Venezuelan recipe and is really vibrant and fresh. It's a fantastic way to use up leftovers from a roast.

BLACK BEAN, AVOCADO & CHICKEN TOSTADAS

1 x 400-g/14-oz. can black beans, drained and rinsed

1 tbsp olive oil

1–2 tsp chipotle paste

12 small tacos or tortillas

200 g/7 oz. shredded white cabbage

1 lime, cut into wedges

AVOCADO & CHICKEN TOPPING

2 avocados, chopped (about 150 g/5^1/$_2$ oz. prepared weight)

finely grated zest and juice of 1 lime

2 tbsp mayonnaise

^{1}/$_2$ tsp sea salt

3 spring onions/scallions, finely chopped

large handful of coriander/ cilantro, leaves chopped, plus extra to garnish

1 green or jalapeño chilli/chile, deseeded and finely chopped, plus extra slices to garnish

200 g/7 oz. shredded, cooked chicken

SERVES 4

For the topping, mash the avocado with the back of a fork in a mixing bowl. Stir in the lime zest and juice, mayonnaise and salt, then stir in the spring onions, coriander and chilli. Stir through the chicken and taste, adding more lime juice and salt as needed.

Place the black beans in a small saucepan with a pinch of salt, the oil, chipotle paste and 1 tablespoon water. Cook over a medium heat for 2–3 minutes, then crush very roughly with a potato masher; set aside off the heat.

You can heat the tacos in a pan or in an oven preheated to 200°C/180°C fan/400°F/Gas 6. Either dry fry in a frying pan/skillet over a high heat for about 1 minute on each side, or brush with a little oil and lay them on a baking tray (not overlapping) and bake for 8–10 minutes, turning halfway. They should be a little crisp.

On to each taco spread some of the black beans, then top with a heap of the avocado and chicken. Garnish with extra sliced chilli, coriander leaves and a little shredded cabbage too. Serve with lime wedges for squeezing over.

COOK'S TIP *The avocado and chicken filling can be prepared several hours in advance. You can also double the recipe to serve more people.*

PULSE SWAP *Black beans are best here, but you could use black eye beans/peas, kidney beans or pinto beans.*

Smashed butter beans should not be confined to this serving suggestion here (although do try it). They are simple, delicious, will keep well in the fridge for 72 hours and can be served with fish and chicken as an alternative to mashed potato or rice.

SMASHED BUTTER BEAN & GARLIC PRAWN TOASTS

2–3 large slices of crusty bread or sourdough
salt and black pepper
lemon wedges, to serve

SMASHED BUTTER BEANS
2 tbsp olive oil
1 shallot, finely diced
1 garlic clove, finely chopped
1 x 400-g/14-oz. can butter/lima beans, drained and rinsed
juice of ¼ lemon

GARLIC PRAWNS
2 tbsp olive oil
1 garlic clove, finely sliced
1 mild red chilli/chile, deseeded and chopped
¼ tsp sweet smoked paprika
150 g/5½ oz. raw peeled king prawns/jumbo shrimp, patted dry on paper towel
juice of ¼ lemon
small handful of flat-leaf parsley, chopped

SERVES 2–3

For the smashed butter beans, heat the oil in a saucepan over a medium-high heat. Fry the shallot and garlic for about 5 minutes until soft and starting to turn golden. Tip in the butter beans, add a pinch of salt and cook gently for 5 minutes. Take off the heat, add the lemon juice and mash with a potato masher; taste and season accordingly. Set aside to cool while you fry the prawns.

For the garlic prawns, heat the oil in frying pan/skillet over a medium-high heat. Fry the garlic and red chilli for 30 seconds. Add the paprika, prawns and a good pinch of salt and fry for 3 minutes, stirring regularly, until the prawns are pink and cooked through. Squeeze over the lemon juice, sprinkle in the parsley and then take the pan off the heat.

Toast the bread or sourdough. You can do this simply in a toaster, or if you want to pull out the stops, drizzle with a little olive oil and rub with the cut side of a garlic clove, then griddle or grill/broil until lightly charred.

Spread the smashed butter beans generously over the toast, then spoon over the prawns and their cooking oil. Serve immediately with lemon wedges.

COOK'S TIP *The smashed butter beans should be quite a stiff consistency when served. You can add a tablespoon of the bean liquid or water if it's looking too thick. If you make the beans in advance and chill them, then you may also need to loosen with a splash of water and aim to serve them at room temperature.*

Pulses, in general, don't boast a lot of flavour in their own right so it makes sense to pair them with anything bold and punchy. Here salty sun-dried tomatoes and olives, peppery rocket and tangy blue cheese are welcome bedfellows.

LENTIL CHOPPED SALAD

2 tbsp olive oil (ideally extra virgin)
1 tbsp balsamic vinegar
250 g/9 oz. cooked brown lentils, drained and rinsed
1 carrot, peeled and finely diced
50 g/scant 1/2 cup stoned/pitted black olives, roughly chopped
50 g/1/2 cup sun-dried tomatoes, roughly chopped
large handful of wild rocket/arugula, baby spinach or fresh soft herbs (parsley or basil), roughly chopped
80 g/3 oz. gorgonzola cheese
salt and black pepper

SERVES 2

In a mixing bowl, whisk together the oil and balsamic with a grind of black pepper. Toss in the lentils to coat in the oil and vinegar.

Add the carrot, olives, sun-dried tomatoes and rocket and toss everything together. Taste and season with salt and pepper as desired.

Serve either with the gorgonzola on the side, or cut into small pieces and scattered on top.

COOK'S TIP *The beauty of this salad is that you can added pretty much anything you like, as long as it's chopped up. Diced avocado, cucumber, celery and red (bell) peppers would all be happy in the mix.*

I am well aware that a can of lentils can feel underwhelming. My solution is to fry them in a little oil and garlic to give them a bit of oomph.

FRIED LENTILS, RICOTTA & PROSCIUTTO

2 tbsp extra virgin olive oil, plus extra to serve
1 garlic clove, crushed or finely grated
250 g/9 oz. cooked beluga or Puy/French lentils, drained and rinsed
250 g/generous 1 cup ricotta
grated zest of 1 lemon
small handful of basil leaves, shredded
150 g/5 1/2 oz. cherry tomatoes, halved
50 g/1 cup wild rocket/arugula
8 slices prosciutto
balsamic vinegar, to serve
salt and black pepper

SERVES 4 AS AN APPETIZER OR 2 AS A MAIN COURSE

Heat the oil in a large frying pan/skillet over a medium-high heat. Add the garlic and fry for 30 seconds, then add the lentils and a pinch of salt. Fry, stirring regularly, for 3–4 minutes, then set aside off the heat.

Mix the ricotta, lemon zest, basil and some salt and pepper. Divide between plates and top with the tomatoes, rocket, prosciutto and lentils. Drizzle with a little more oil and some balsamic vinegar to serve.

COOK'S TIP *For a vegetarian option, replace the prosciutto for grilled strips of aubergine/eggplant or chargrilled artichoke hearts.*

Pictured on page 51

The crispy chickpeas, dressing and avocado are the stars here, so feel free to adapt the rest of the salad ingredients as you like. Any leaves will work, and you could add some cherry tomatoes or roasted chunks of sweet potato, too. You could even leave out the leaves and serve it all on rice or noodles if you want something a bit more filling

CRISPY CHICKPEA & AVOCADO SALAD
with tahini-miso dressing

150 g/5¹/2 oz. bitter leaves (such as chicory/endive, radicchio, watercress or rocket/arugula)
1 carrot, julienned or grated/shredded
1 ripe avocado, halved and sliced
sea salt
toasted sesame seeds, to serve

CRISPY CHICKPEAS
1 x 400-g/14-oz. can chickpeas/garbanzo beans, drained and rinsed
2 tbsp olive oil
finely grated zest of ¹/2 lemon
¹/2 tsp ground cumin

TAHINI-MISO DRESSING
2 tbsp tahini
1 tbsp white miso paste
1 tbsp soy sauce
2 tsp maple syrup
2 tsp rice vinegar
¹/2 tsp grated fresh root ginger

SERVES 2

For the crispy chickpeas, rinse the chickpeas and tip onto a clean tea towel. Pat dry as best you can. If any skins come off, discard them. Heat the oil in a frying pan/skillet over a medium-high heat. Fry the chickpeas for 8–10 minutes, shaking the pan regularly, until golden and turning crisp. Add a good pinch of sea salt, the lemon zest and cumin and continue cooking for a couple of minutes until deep golden; set aside off the heat.

Meanwhile, mix all the ingredients for the tahini-miso dressing with 1–2 tablespoons cold water. It should be about the consistency of single/light cream, so add more water if needed.

Arrange the chicory, carrot and avocado on plates (or a serving platter). Spoon over some of the dressing (you may not need it all), then tumble over the crispy chickpeas. Finish with some toasted sesame seeds.

COOK'S TIP *I've cooked crispy chickpeas in the oven and on the hob/stovetop, and I think this is the best method for both speed and crunch. I would say a queen chickpea (for example from Bold Bean Co) is perfect for this recipe. Make sure to dry them as best you can before frying or they'll pop and splutter even more in the pan.*

This is real warm-weather food, a version of it first made for me by my friend Gemma who lives in Ibiza and dresses it simply with olive oil and lemon juice. The anchovy dressing gives it a bit of pizzazz, although either option is great. I challenge any celery haters (I know there are a lot of you out there) not to enjoy this salad.

TUNA, BUTTER BEAN & CELERY SALAD with anchovy dressing

150 g/5¹/2 oz. tuna (canned
    or jarred, drained weight)
    in spring water or olive oil
4 celery stalks/ribs, trimmed
    and quite thinly sliced, plus
    any leaves reserved to garnish
1 x 400-g/14-oz. can butter/lima
    beans, drained and rinsed
¹/2 red onion, finely diced
2 hard-boiled/hard-cooked eggs,
    chopped

ANCHOVY DRESSING
4 anchovy fillets, chopped
4 tbsp extra virgin olive oil
2 tbsp red wine vinegar
2 small garlic cloves, crushed
salt and black pepper

SERVES 2

Drain the tuna. If it is in olive oil, then use this in the dressing instead of the same quantity of olive oil. Roughly flake the tuna and add to a bowl with the celery, butter beans and red onion.

In a small high-speed blender, whizz the anchovies, oil, vinegar and garlic with a good grind of black pepper until smooth. If needed add a small pinch of salt, although remember the anchovies are very salty in themselves.

Toss about half of the dressing through the salad, adding more to taste. Finally stir through the chopped eggs. Divide between plates, scatter with any reserved celery leaves and serve.

COOK'S TIP *If you find raw red onion a little too pungent, then place the diced onion in a bowl and cover with cold water. Leave for 5 minutes, then drain. It'll just take the edge off it.*

PULSE SWAP *Cannellini or kidney beans would be great in this summery salad.*

This is inspired by the American side dish of succotash, which is an ode to summer vegetables and usually includes sweetcorn, fresh broad/fava beans and red (bell) peppers. Here I've swapped the broad beans for black eyed beans/peas, although you could use a mix of the two in early summer when the young broad beans are in season.

COD, BLACK EYED BEANS & SWEETCORN

4 x 120-g/4-oz. skinless cod fillets (or another firm white fish like hake or pollock)
1 tbsp olive oil
100 g/3¹/₂ oz. smoked bacon lardons (or diced pancetta)
1 onion, finely diced
1 red (bell) pepper, deseeded and diced
250 g/1³/₄ cups sweetcorn (from a can or frozen)
1 x 400-g/14-oz. can black eyed beans/peas, drained and rinsed
100 ml/scant ¹/₂ cup white wine
100 ml/scant ¹/₂ cup chicken stock
5 tbsp single/light cream
juice of ¹/₂ lemon
large handful of chopped flat-leaf parsley
salt

SERVES 4

Take the cod out of the fridge 20 minutes before you want to cook it and season lightly with salt; set aside.

Meanwhile, heat the oil over a medium-high heat in a large frying or sauté pan/skillet for which you have a lid. Fry the bacon and onion, stirring regularly, for 8 minutes until starting to turn golden.

Stir in the red pepper, corn and black eyed beans and fry for another 2 minutes. Add the wine and simmer briskly until it has almost completely bubbled off, then add the stock and simmer until reduced by half.

Stir in the cream and bring to a gentle simmer. Nestle the cod fillets in the pan, then squeeze over the lemon juice, cover with a lid and cook for 8–10 minutes, or until the fish is cooked through. Scatter over the chopped parsley, then divide among shallow bowls to serve.

COOK'S TIP *You could use any firm white fish, like hake or pollock, in this recipe. Or you can skip the fish and just serve the beans with grilled/broiled chicken or lamb.*

PULSE SWAP *Kidney beans or cannellini beans would be a good swap for black eyed beans.*

I love basmati's delicate fragrant grains, making this an elegant baked rice dish. It's great for popping down on the table and letting everyone dig in.

BAKED CHICKPEAS & RICE with artichokes

200 g/1¼ cups white
   basmati rice
2 tbsp olive oil
2 onions, diced
1 tsp sea salt
2 garlic cloves, finely chopped
1 red (bell) pepper, deseeded
   and cut into thin strips
1 heaped tbsp tomato
   purée/paste
1 tsp sweet smoked paprika
1 x 400-g/14-oz. can chickpeas/
   garbanzo beans, drained
   and rinsed
juice of ½ lemon
500 ml/2 cups vegetable stock
200 g/7 oz. chargrilled
   artichoke hearts

TO SERVE
lemon wedges
green salad
garlic mayonnaise or aïoli
   (plant-based if necessary)

SERVES 4

Preheat the oven to 200°C/180°C fan/400°F/Gas 6. Place the rice in a mixing bowl, cover with cold water, then agitate the grains with your hand. Pour off the cloudy water and repeat the process twice more, or until the water is no longer cloudy. Leave the rice to soak in cold water.

Heat the oil over a medium-high heat in a large ovenproof sauté pan or shallow casserole. Fry the onions with ½ teaspoon salt for 5 minutes until starting to soften. Add the garlic and red pepper and fry, stirring regularly, for another 5–7 minutes until golden.

Add the tomato purée and paprika and fry, stirring, for 2 minutes. Drain the rice and add to the pan along with the chickpeas, another ½ teaspoon salt and the lemon juice, stirring everything together over the heat. Pour in the stock and bring everything to a brisk simmer. Cook for 2 minutes, then arrange the artichokes over the top. Transfer the pan to the oven and bake for 30–35 minutes until golden and crispy on top.

Take the pan out of the oven and leave to stand for 10 minutes. Serve with lemon wedges, a green salad and (plant-based) garlic mayonnaise or aïoli.

COOK'S TIP *This is a plant-based dish, but you could scatter some cubes of feta or halloumi over the top halfway through cooking to jazz it up if it suits your dietary needs.*

PULSE SWAP *Replace the chickpeas with butter/lima beans or black beans.*

ONE PAN

Meatballs are the epitome of comfort food and here they are wrapped in a blanket of a tomato and mascarpone sauce with nutty borlotti beans. I can think of nothing better to serve them with than garlic bread and a green salad. By all means buy readymade meatballs if you're short on time.

CHICKEN & SAGE MEATBALLS with borlotti

1 large onion
5 sage leaves
500 g/1 lb. 2 oz. minced/ground chicken, ideally dark thigh meat (see cook's tip)
1/2 tsp salt
1 tbsp olive oil
2 garlic cloves, crushed
1 x 400-g/14-oz. can chopped tomatoes
150 ml/2/3 cup chicken stock
1 x 400-g/14-oz. can borlotti/ cranberry beans, drained and rinsed
pinch of sugar
2 tbsp mascarpone
black pepper
Crispy sage leaves, to serve (optional; see cook's tip page 25)

SERVES 4

Grate the onion on the coarse side of a box grater. Place half in a mixing bowl and set the other half aside. To the mixing bowl add 5 finely chopped sage leaves, the chicken and the salt. Add a good grind of black pepper. Mix together with your hands and shape into 12 meatballs.

Heat the oil in a large sauté pan or shallow casserole. Add the meatballs and fry for about 8 minutes, turning regularly until browned all over. Lift out of the pan and set aside.

Keep the pan on the heat (there should be enough fat left in it for frying, if not add a splash more) and fry the reserved grated onion and the garlic with a pinch of salt for 5 minutes until soft. Add the chopped tomatoes, stock, beans and a pinch of sugar. Season with salt and pepper and lower the meatballs back into the pan.

Simmer gently for 15–20 minutes, turning the meatballs every so often. Take off the heat and stir the mascarpone into the sauce. Serve scattered with crispy sage leaves to finish, if liked.

COOK'S TIP *You can make these meatballs with your choice of mince. I like to use chicken (my butcher minces the thigh meat for me) but I have also made them with pork or veal (10–15 per cent fat), which both work well. I'd avoid any really 'lean' mince options as they can dry out a bit during cooking.*

PULSE SWAP *Try using flageolet, haricot/navy or butter/lima beans instead of borlotti beans.*

It is thanks to brilliant Indian restaurant Dishoom that many Brits fell in love with black dal. Also known as dal makhani, it is traditionally made with urid black lentils, which require overnight soaking and plenty of boiling time. This is a speedy version using canned lentils and it is as characteristically indulgent and heart-warming as the original.

QUICK BLACK DAL

1 onion
40 g/2^1/$_2$ tbsp unsalted butter
2 garlic cloves, finely grated
1^1/$_2$ tsp finely grated fresh
    root ginger
1^1/$_2$ tsp garam masala
1 tsp mild chilli/chile powder
60 g/4 tablespoons tomato
    purée/paste
1 tsp honey
1 x 400-g/14-oz. can beluga
    lentils, drained and rinsed
^{1}/$_2$ x 400-g/14-oz. can red kidney
    beans, drained and rinsed
^{1}/$_2$ tsp salt
3 tbsp single/light cream,
    plus a splash more to serve
a squeeze of lemon juice
    (optional) black pepper

TO SERVE
coriander/cilantro leaves
sliced chilli/chile
rice or bread

SERVES 3–4

Grate the onion on the coarse side of a box grater, stopping when you get to the root. Heat the butter in a large saucepan over a medium-high heat and fry the grated onion with a pinch of salt for 5 minutes. Add the garlic and ginger and fry for 2 minutes more.

Stir in the spices, cooking for a minute, then add the tomato purée. Cook, stirring constantly, for a couple of minutes until it darkens a little but making sure it doesn't catch on the bottom of the pan.

Add 200 ml/scant 1 cup water, the honey, lentils, kidney beans, salt and a good grind of black pepper. Simmer for 10 minutes, then stir in the cream. Season with more salt and a perhaps a squeeze of lemon juice if needed. Serve with a splash more cream, some coriander leaves and sliced fresh chilli if liked. Steamed rice and naan or chapatis are great too.

COOK'S TIP *Grating an onion on a box grater is a great way to get a pulpy texture (a bit like you would achieve in a food processor). I also like to prepare onions in this way to add to minced/ground meat for meatballs and koftes.*

PULSE SWAP *Use Puy/French or brown lentils instead of beluga.*

A humble Greek dish that's brimming with flavour and can be served as a meal in its own right, or makes a great side to roast chicken or lamb. I like to eat it with crusty bread and soft, fresh cheese, such as ricotta or goat's cheese.

BLACK EYED BEANS & SPINACH

4 tbsp extra virgin olive oil, plus more to serve
1 onion, finely diced
2 garlic cloves, finely chopped
1 heaped tsp tomato purée/ paste
1 large tomato (about 150 g/ 5¹/₂ oz.), finely chopped
¹/₂ x 400-g/14-oz. can black eyed beans/peas, drained and rinsed
400 g/8 cups fresh spinach
salt
crusty bread, to serve

SERVES 4

Heat 2 tablespoons of the oil in a large frying pan/skillet over a medium-high heat. Fry the onion, garlic and a good pinch of salt for about 8 minutes until soft and turning golden. Add the tomato purée and fry for a couple of minutes until it darkens and caramelizes a little, then add the fresh tomato and fry for a minute more.

Stir in the beans. Add the spinach a handful at a time, stirring until it has wilted before adding more. Tip in 150 ml/²/₃ cup water and remaining 2 tablespoons oil, season and bring to a simmer and cook for 10 minutes until the liquid has reduced a bit but it's still nice and saucy. Drizzle with a splash more oil and serve with crusty bread, if you like.

COOK'S TIP *This is adaptable to what's in the fridge. Fry some chopped carrots or (bell) peppers with the onion and use a mix of greens – say half spring greens, half spinach. You can also add some fresh herbs if you have them – parsley, thyme and oregano would all go well.*

Sausages and lentils are a classic combination, although you'll most commonly find firm green or Puy/French lentils used in recipes. I've used red lentils here and they work brilliantly well, cooking down to an almost mash-like consistency which, as we know, is a popular pairing for sausages. The nuggets of onion marmalade melt into the sauce and add a little sweetness in the place of an onion gravy.

BRAISED SAUSAGES, RED LENTILS & CARAMELIZED ONIONS

200 g/1 cup dried red lentils,
rinsed (see cook's tip)
2 tbsp olive oil
8 sausages
1 large onion, finely diced
1 large garlic clove, finely
chopped
500 ml/2 cups chicken
or vegetable stock
6 thyme sprigs
2 tbsp caramelized onion
marmalade (shop-bought
is fine)
salt
steamed greens and mustard,
to serve (optional)

SERVES 4

Preheat the oven to 180°C/160°C fan/350°F/Gas 4. Place the rinsed lentils in a bowl of cold water to soak.

Meanwhile, heat the oil over a medium-high heat in a large ovenproof sauté pan or shallow casserole. Add the sausages and fry, turning regularly, for 6-8 minutes until golden in places. Lift out of the pan and set aside.

Add the onion, garlic and a pinch of salt to the pan, lower the heat to medium and cook for 8–10 minutes until softened and just turning golden. Drain the lentils and add to the pan with the stock and the thyme springs. Bring to the boil, then simmer briskly for 5 minutes.

Dot small teaspoons of the onion marmalade around the pan. Nestle in the sausages and transfer the pan to the oven. Cook for 35 minutes, then stand for 5 minutes before serving with steamed greens and mustard, if you like.

COOK'S TIP *To rinse the lentils, place in a mixing bowl and cover with cold water, then agitate the lentils with your hands. Pour off the cloudy water and repeat the process two more times, or until the water is no longer cloudy.*

This is chilli con carne's lighter cousin and the perfect way to use up leftover chicken from a roast; although I'll often pick up a rotisserie chicken on the way home just to make this.

WHITE BEAN CHILLI CHICKEN

2 tbsp olive oil
1 onion, diced
4 garlic cloves, finely chopped
2 green or jalapeño chillies/
  chiles, 1 finely chopped and
  1 sliced (deseeded if liked)
large handful of coriander/
  cilantro, stalks finely chopped
  and leaves to garnish
1½ tsp ground cumin
1 tsp ground coriander
¼ tsp cayenne pepper
1 x 400-g/14-oz. can cannellini
  beans, drained and rinsed
350 ml/1½ cups chicken stock
juice of 1 lime
400 g/14 oz. shredded, cooked
  chicken
4–5 tbsp soured cream

TO SERVE
sliced avocado
grated Cheddar
tortilla chips

SERVES 4

Heat the oil in a large sauté or frying pan/skillet over a medium-high heat. Fry the onion and garlic with a pinch of salt for about 8–10 minutes until soft and turning golden. Add the chopped chilli, chopped coriander stalks and spices and fry for 2 minutes more.

Stir the beans into the pan, then add the stock and simmer for 4–5 minutes until reduced by half. Stir in the juice of ½ lime and the shredded chicken, then stir in the soured cream. Taste, season with salt and lime juice as needed, then simmer for a minute more.

To serve, pile into bowls (with or without rice) and top with the sliced chilli, coriander leaves, sliced avocado and grated Cheddar. Serve with tortillas chips on the side.

COOK'S TIP *If you have chicken skin that needs using up (from leftovers or a rotisserie chicken), shred it and fry with the onions for extra flavour.*

PULSE SWAP *Any white bean (such as butter/lima or haricot/navy) would work in this recipe, or you could use kidney beans or even black eyed beans/peas.*

This makes an elegant, quick supper for two. I love the colourful stalks of rainbow chard, but you could use any leafy greens here.

GREENS, BEANS & WHITE FISH

2 x 120-g /4¹/₂-oz. skinless firm white fish fillets (hake, cod or pollock)
2 tbsp olive oil
1 onion, halved and thinly sliced
2 garlic cloves, finely chopped
4 anchovies, finely chopped (optional)
200 g/7 oz. rainbow chard, leaves and stalks separated
150 ml/²/₃ cup white wine
100 ml/scant ¹/₂ cup chicken, vegetable or fish stock
1 x 400-g/14-oz. can butter/lima beans, drained (reserving the liquid, see below)
100 ml/scant ¹/₂ cup of the bean liquid (see cook's tip)
3 tbsp double/heavy cream
juice of ¹/₂ lemon
salt
handful of dill leaves, to garnish

SERVES 2

Take the fish out the fridge and season lightly with salt; set aside.

Meanwhile, heat the oil over a medium-high heat in a large frying or sauté pan/skillet for which you have a lid. Fry the onion, garlic and anchovies (if using) with a good pinch of salt, stirring regularly, for 3–4 minutes until starting to soften.

Cut the chard stalks into 4-cm/1¹/₂-inch lengths and add to the pan, frying for another 3–4 minutes. Add the wine and simmer until reduced by half, then add the stock and again reduce the liquid by half.

Add the beans and bean liquid and the cream, then shred the chard leaves and add them to the pan. Bring to a very gentle simmer, then nestle in the fish fillets. Squeeze over the lemon juice, cover the pan with a lid and cook gently for 8 minutes, or until the fish is cooked through.

Scatter over the dill, divide between shallow bowls and serve.

COOK'S TIP *Ideally use beans that are canned or jarred in water only (with no salt or preservatives), or reserve some of the cooking liquid if cooking from dried.*

PULSE SWAP *Cannellini, haricot/navy or black eyed beans/peas would be great here.*

Chorizo is a great companion to any pulse. Here its silky, spicy red oil cloaks mellow black beans and short-grain rice to make a dish that is full-blown comfort food. Unbeatable topped with a poached or soft-boiled egg.

CHORIZO & BLACK BEAN RICE

1 tbsp olive oil
1 onion, diced
200 g/7 oz. cooking chorizo, diced
1 x 400-g/14-oz. can black beans, drained and rinsed
250 g/1¼ cups paella rice
600 ml/2½ cups chicken or vegetable stock, heated
100 g/3½ oz. cavolo nero, leaves stripped from stalks and roughly torn
juice of ½ lemon
salt
4 poached or soft-boiled/soft-cooked eggs, to serve (optional)

SERVES 4

Preheat the oven to 200°C/180°C fan/400°F/Gas 6.

Heat the oil in a large, ovenproof frying pan/skillet over a medium-high heat. Add the onion and a pinch of salt and fry for 5 minutes until starting to soften. Add the chorizo and fry for another 5 minutes. Stir in the beans and the rice.

Pour over the hot stock. Bring to a brisk simmer and cook for about 5 minutes. Stir in the cavolo nero and squeeze over the lemon juice. Transfer to the oven and bake for 25 minutes.

Remove from the oven and stand for 5 minutes. Serve in bowls. It is wonderful as is, or can be topped with a poached egg if you like.

COOK'S TIP *Paella rice works best in this dish, but you could also use arborio rice or a short- or medium-grain pudding rice.*

PULSE SWAP *Aduki beans are a good swap for black beans, otherwise try butter/lima beans, kidney beans or black beluga lentils.*

SRI LANKAN-STYLE RED LENTIL DAL

200 g/generous 1 cup red split lentils
1 tbsp coconut or vegetable oil
1 shallot, finely chopped
1 garlic clove, finely chopped
1 green chilli/chile, finely chopped (deseeded, if liked)
small handful of fresh curry leaves
1½ tsp mild curry powder
½ tsp turmeric
½ tsp salt
1 small cinnamon stick or pinch of ground cinnamon (optional)
1 x 400-ml/14-oz. can coconut milk
rice, lime wedges and coriander/cilantro leaves, to serve

SERVES 4

Start by rinsing the lentils. Place in a mixing bowl and cover with cold water, then agitate the lentils with your hands. Pour off the cloudy water and repeat the process two more times, or until the water is no longer cloudy.

Heat the oil in a saucepan over a medium-high heat. Add the shallot and garlic and fry for 3–4 minutes, then add the chilli and curry leaves and fry for 2 minutes more. Add the curry powder, turmeric, salt and cinnamon and stir over the heat for a minute, then add the drained lentils, coconut milk and 250 ml/1 cup water.

Bring to the boil, lower to a simmer and cook for 25–30 minutes, or until the lentils are completely tender. Taste and add more salt if needed. Serve with rice, lime wedges and coriander.

COOK'S TIP *For an extra green boost you can add some green veg to this for the last 5 minutes of cooking. Try frozen peas or fresh spinach. It's also nice with roasted cubes of squash added before serving.*

Pictured on page 77

I first wrote this recipe for Waitrose magazine back in 2018 and it was hugely popular. It was taught to me by a wonderful cook called Prem who ran a little restaurant in Tangalle, Sri Lanka. She would simply toss all the ingredients in a pot and simmer until the lentils were tender, and it was just delicious. I still use this method when I'm short on time, otherwise I fry the aromatics first, as here, for a slightly more nuanced flavour.

This is a sensational roasting tin recipe. I like to crush the butter beans on my plate with a fork and allow them to soak up all the wonderful cooking juices.

TRAYBAKED CHICKEN & BUTTER
BEANS with olives & lemon

6 large chicken thighs
   (skin-on and bone-in), about
   150 g/5 oz. each
100 g/1 cup stoned/pitted green
   olives, drained
5 fresh oregano sprigs
3 garlic cloves, crushed
2 tbsp red wine vinegar
2 tbsp small capers, such
   as nonpareille, drained
2 tbsp runny honey
1 tbsp olive oil
1/2 tsp salt
100 ml/scant 1/2 cup white wine
2 x 400-g/14-oz. cans butter/
   lima beans, drained and rinsed
1/2 small lemon, sliced
black pepper

SERVES 6

Start by marinating the chicken. Place the thighs in a large bowl or resealable food bag with the olives, oregano, garlic, vinegar, capers, honey, oil and salt. Add a good grind of black pepper and mix everything together so the chicken is well coated. Set aside for at least 1 hour, or ideally up to 12 hours.

Preheat the oven to 190°C/170°C fan/375°F/Gas 5. In a large roasting tin, arrange the chicken, skin-side up, with its marinade. Pour over the white wine. Roast for about 40 minutes, basting the chicken in the cooking juices halfway through.

After 40 minutes, remove the dish from the oven. Baste the chicken again and add the butter beans and lemon slices to the sauce. Return to the oven for a final 15–20 minutes. Stand for 10 minutes to allow the chicken to rest before serving.

COOK'S TIP *This doesn't necessarily need a starchy carbohydrate with it (a green salad will do nicely), although you could serve it with couscous or rice if you're feeding a crowd.*

PULSE SWAP *I think plump butter beans are best here, but you could use cannellini too.*

TO SHARE

These braised black beans are a take on a Cuban recipe, traditionally made with dried beans but using canned speeds things up dramatically. They make a fantastic vegetarian meal served with rice, sliced avocado and a dollop of yogurt. For something a bit more special, top it with chunks of melting pork belly.

CUBAN-STYLE BLACK BEANS
with crispy pork belly

PORK BELLY
juice of 1 orange
zest and juice of 1 unwaxed lime
3 garlic cloves, crushed
1 tsp ground coriander
1 tsp dried oregano
1 tsp honey
³/₄ tsp salt
500 g/1 lb. 2 oz. pork belly slices
black pepper

BLACK BEANS
2 tbsp olive oil
1 onion, finely diced
1 green (bell) pepper, deseeded
    and finely diced
2 garlic cloves, crushed
handful of coriander/cilantro,
    stalks finely chopped
1 tsp ground cumin
¹/₂ tsp dried oregano
2 x 400-g/14-oz. cans black
    beans, drained and rinsed
250 ml/1 cup chicken
    or vegetable stock
juice of 1 lime
salt

TO SERVE
cooked rice
lime wedges

SERVES 4

If making the pork belly, aim to marinate it at least 2–4 hours in advance. Combine all the ingredients in a bowl or sealable food container with lots of ground black pepper; set aside to marinate.

When ready to cook, preheat the oven to 200°C/180°C fan/400°F/ Gas 6. Line a baking tray with parchment.

Place the pork belly slices on the lined sheet and cover with any marinade from the bowl. Roast for 50 minutes, turning and basting every 15 minutes, until golden and sticky. Rest for about 10 minutes before slicing.

For the beans, heat the oil in a large saucepan over a medium-high heat. Fry the onion, green pepper, garlic and chopped coriander stalks with a big pinch of salt for 6–8 minutes until soft and turning golden. Add the cumin and oregano and fry for a minute more, then add the beans and stock. Simmer for 10 minutes until the beans are coated in a thick sauce.

Season the beans with the lime juice and more salt, if needed. Serve with rice, the sliced pork belly, lime wedges and scatter over the coriander leaves.

COOK'S TIP *You can happily double up this recipe to feed a larger crowd. In which case it might be worth swapping the pork belly slices for a shoulder and slow cooking it in the marinade.*

This is a riff on mujadara, a wonderful Middle Eastern dish of rice, lentils and caramelized onions. Here the onions are roasted in the tin with the chicken, because it is hard to beat the flavour of onions slow-cooked in chicken fat. I tend to serve this with a simple salad of bitter leaves with an oil and vinegar dressing.

SPICED RICE & LENTILS
with roast chicken

1.5-kg/3¼-lb. whole chicken
   (ideally free-range)
2 large red onions, halved
   and thinly sliced
2 large garlic cloves, sliced
1 tbsp olive oil
1 lemon
1 tsp ground cumin
½ tsp ground cinnamon
½ tsp ground allspice
500 g/3¾ cups cooked
   wholegrain rice
250 g/9 oz. cooked green, brown
   or Puy/French lentils
150 g/⅔ cup pomegranate
   seeds
large bunch of coriander/
   cilantro, roughly chopped
large bunch of flat-leaf parsley,
   roughly chopped
salt and black pepper

SERVES 4–6

Take the chicken out of the fridge at least 30 minutes before you plan to cook it. Remove all packaging and season inside and out with salt; set aside until ready to cook.

Preheat the oven to 200°C/180°C fan/400°F/Gas 6. Toss the onions and garlic in the base of a roasting tin with ½ tablespoon of oil and season with salt. Sit the chicken on top of the onions, breast-side down, and roast for 20 minutes.

Meanwhile, thinly slice one-quarter of the lemon.

Remove the tin from the oven, lift the chicken onto a plate, then stir up the onions and garlic adding the sliced lemon. Sit the chicken back on top, breast-side up, drizzle over the remaining ½ tablespoon of oil and grind over some black pepper. Roast for 40 minutes, basting the bird in the cooking juices halfway through.

Check the chicken is cooked (74°C/165°F on a thermometer, or when the juices run clear when a skewer is inserted into the thickest part of the thigh). Transfer to a plate, loosely covered with foil to rest.

Stir the spices into the onions and return to the oven for about 10–12 minutes until golden. Spoon off any excess oil from the tray if necessary, then stir the cooked rice and lentils through the onions and return to the oven for a final 5 minutes to warm through.

Check the seasoning of the rice, adding the juice of the remaining lemon and more salt to taste. Stir through the pomegranate seeds and herbs and transfer to a serving platter. Carve the chicken and arrange the pieces on top, spooning over any resting juices.

COOK'S TIP *You can buy handy pouches of ready-cooked rice, but if you want to cook from dried you will need 225 g/generous 1 cup.*

PULSE SWAP *Any soft green or brown lentils will work here.*

Quesadillas are toasted tortillas filled with cheese, a bit like a Mexican-style cheese toastie. They can have any number of additional fillings and this is a fabulous option. Pinto are soft, creamy beans that are commonly used in Mexico to make refried beans and making your own couldn't be easier (and taste much better than anything pre-made from a can).

PRAWN, PINTO BEAN & KIMCHI QUESADILLAS

3 large tortilla wraps
4–5 tbsp kimchi
100 g/generous 1 cup
    Cheddar cheese,
    grated/shredded
salt
salsa and guacamole,
    to serve (optional)

PINTO 'REFRIED' BEANS
2 tbsp olive oil
1 echalion/banana shallot
    or small onion, diced
2 garlic cloves, chopped
3/4 tsp ground cumin
3/4 tsp mild chilli/chile
    powder
1 x 400-g/14-oz. can pinto
    beans, drained and
    rinsed

LIME & HONEY PRAWNS
1 tbsp olive oil
170 g/1 1/3 cups peeled raw
    king prawns/jumbo
    shrimp
juice of 1 lime
2 tsp runny honey

SERVES 2 AS A MAIN
OR 3–4 AS A SNACK

Start by making the beans. Heat the oil in a large saucepan over a medium-high heat. Fry the shallot or onion and garlic with a pinch of salt for 6–8 minutes until turning golden. Add the spices and cook for 2 minutes more. Add the beans and 100 ml/scant 1/2 cup water and simmer briskly for 2–3 minutes until most of the liquid has evaporated, then crush with a potato masher and set aside to cool.

For the prawns, heat the oil over a high heat in a large frying pan/skillet. Pat the prawns dry on a paper towel, season with salt, then add to the pan. Fry for a minute on each side, then add the lime juice and honey and stir-fry over the heat for a final minute until they are cooked through and charred in places. Set aside on a plate.

Clean out the large frying pan and set over a medium heat. To build the quesadillas, set the tortillas out on a work surface. Spread half of each with the beans. Next, divide the prawns between the tortillas arranging them on top of the beans. Scatter with the kimchi and the cheese.

Fold the tortillas in half so the fillings are encased, then add to the hot pan (you may be able to cook two at a time, or just do one for ease of flipping). Fry for 1–2 minutes on each side until just a little golden and the cheese has melted. Cut into wedges and serve with salsa and guacamole, if you like.

COOK'S TIP *You can make the refried beans in advance. If using from chilled, you may need to add a splash of warm water to loosen them. They are also brilliant in burritos, as a dip served with nachos or in breakfast tacos with scrambled eggs and fried chorizo.*

PULSE SWAP *Make the refried beans with black beans or kidney beans.*

KIDGEREE

200 g/1¹/₄ cups basmati rice

40 g/3 tablespoons unsalted butter

1 onion, finely diced

¹/₂ tsp salt

1 heaped tsp mild curry powder

¹/₄ tsp ground turmeric

4 cardamom pods, roughly cracked

1 cinnamon stick

1 bay leaf

1 x 400-g/14 oz. can red kidney beans, drained and rinsed

350 ml/1¹/₃ cups chicken, fish or vegetable stock

juice of ¹/₂ lemon

4 eggs

a handful of chopped coriander/cilantro

black pepper

lemon wedges, to serve

SERVES 4

Place the rice in a mixing bowl, cover with cold water, then agitate the grains with your hand. Pour off the cloudy water and repeat the process twice more, or until the water is clear. Leave the rice to soak in cold water.

Heat the butter in a large saucepan or shallow casserole (for which you have a tight-fitting lid) over a medium heat. Add the onion and salt and fry, stirring, for 5 minutes until soft. Add the spices and bay leaf and fry for a minute more.

Drain the rice and stir into the pan, frying for a minute, then add the kidney beans and stock. Squeeze over the juice of ¹/₂ lemon and grind over some black pepper. Bring to the boil, then lower to a gentle simmer and cover with the lid. Cook for 12 minutes, then take off the heat and leave, covered, for another 10 minutes.

While the rice rests, bring a separate saucepan of water to the boil. Lower in the eggs and boil for 7 minutes for jammy yolks. Drain and run under the cold tap to cool, then peel and quarter.

Fluff the rice with a fork and season to taste. Stir through the coriander leaves, then pile onto plates and top with the quartered boiled eggs and lemon wedges on the side.

COOK'S TIP *No one likes chomping on a whole cardamom pod, so remove the whole spices before serving.*

PULSE SWAP *Replace the kidney beans with chickpeas/garbanzo beans or black beans.*

This all gets cooked over two shelves of the oven in about 30 minutes. The colours are deep and vibrant and the flavours are gloriously punchy.

ROASTED CARROTS, LENTIL & GRAPE SALAD

750 g/1 lb. 10 oz. carrots, rinsed and cut into spears
6 tbsp extra virgin olive oil
500 g/3 cups Puy/ French, beluga, green or brown lentils
250 g/³⁄₄ cup seedless red grapes
2 small red onions, halved and sliced
2 tbsp balsamic vinegar
1¹⁄₂ tsp runny honey
200 g/7 oz. soft goat's cheese
large handful of flat-leaf parsley, leaves shredded
salt and black pepper

SERVES 4–6

Preheat the oven to 220°C/200°C fan/425°F/Gas 7. Arrange two shelves in the oven, one at the top and one in the middle. Toss the carrots with 2 tablespoons of the oil, season and spread out over a roasting tray. Roast on the top shelf for about 15 minutes, stirring halfway.

In a separate large roasting tin, stir the lentils, grapes, onions, vinegar, honey together with the remaining 4 tablespoons of the oil. Season with salt and pepper.

Give the carrots a stir and transfer to the middle shelf. Put the tray of lentils on the top shelf. Roast for 10 minutes, then remove the carrots and set aside. Stir up the lentils and return to the oven for a final 5 minutes.

Arrange the lentils and carrots over a serving platter. Scatter with the goat's cheese and chopped parsley. Serve immediately.

COOK'S TIP *You can halve the quantities of this recipe to make a meat-free dinner for two.*

Chaat is an Indian street food often found in the appetizer section at Indian restaurants. It's full of tang and texture, and this simplified version certainly packs a punch.

CHAAT-STYLE CHICKPEAS & CAULIFLOWER

1 medium cauliflower
1 x 400-g/14-oz. can chickpeas/garbanzo beans, drained and rinsed
2 tbsp olive oil
1 tsp garam masala
¹⁄₂ tsp salt
3 tbsp lemon juice
2¹⁄₂ tsp chaat masala (see cook's tip)
¹⁄₂ red onion, diced
150 g/5 oz. cucumber, diced
large handful of coriander/cilantro, leaves picked
100 g/scant ¹⁄₂ cup natural/plain yogurt

TAMARIND SAUCE
2 tbsp tamarind paste
1 tsp runny honey

SERVES 4

Preheat the oven to 220°C/200°C fan/425°F/ Gas 7. Trim the cauliflower, reserving any tender leaves, then cut into medium florets. Toss the florets and chickpeas in a large mixing bowl with the oil, garam masala and salt, then spread over a large roasting tray. Roast for 15 minutes, then stir everything and add the cauliflower leaves to the tray. Roast for another 10–15 minutes, or until golden. Set aside to cool for 10 minutes.

Meanwhile, make the tamarind sauce by combining the ingredients. You may need to add a splash of water to loosen it. Set aside.

Combine the lemon juice, chaat masala, onion and cucumber in a large mixing bowl. Toss in the cauliflower, chickpeas and most of the coriander leaves, then tumble onto a large platter. Spoon over the yogurt, then the tamarind sauce, then scatter with the remaining coriander.

COOK'S TIP *Chaat masala is an Indian spice mix available in many major supermarkets now.*

ROASTED TOMATO PIYAZ
with za'atar salmon

**400 g/14 oz. cherry tomatoes,
  halved**
3 tbsp olive oil
½ small red onion, thinly sliced
**2 x 400-g/14-oz. cans cannellini
  beans, drained and rinsed**
4 x 130-g/4½-oz. salmon fillets
juice of 1 small lemon
2 tsp za'atar
2 tsp sumac
**handful of flat-leaf parsley,
  leaves roughly chopped**
salt and black pepper

SERVES 2

Preheat the oven to 220°C/200°C fan/425°F/Gas 7. Stir the tomatoes with 1 tablespoon of the oil and a good pinch of salt in a roasting tin. Roast for 5 minutes.

Meanwhile, soak the sliced onion in a bowl of cold water. This just takes the edge off the raw flavour.

Stir the beans into the tray with the tomatoes, then nestle in the salmon fillets. Drizzle everything with the remaining oil, the lemon juice and season with salt and pepper. Scatter the za'atar over the top of the salmon and the sumac over the tomatoes and beans. Return to the oven for 8 minutes, or until the salmon is cooked.

Drain the onion and stir through the tomatoes and beans. Scatter with the parsley and serve immediately.

COOK'S TIP *You can happily halve this recipe to serve two.*

PULSE SWAP *Try butter/lima beans instead of cannellini.*

This makes a fabulous autumnal/fall salad that always gets a lot of compliments. I sometimes scatter toasted chopped nuts (hazelnuts or pecans) over the top for a bit of crunch. Serve as part of a sharing table, or as a side to steak or roast chicken.

ROASTED SQUASH, CHICORY & BUTTER BEANS with black garlic dressing

1 kg/2¼ lb. butternut squash, peeled, deseeded and cut into 1-cm/½-inch thick wedges
4 tbsp olive oil
4 red chicory/endive bulbs (about 400 g/14 oz.), ends trimmed and cut lengthways into wedges
4 echalion/banana shallots, ends trimmed and cut lengthways into wedges
1 x 400-g/14-oz. can butter/lima beans, drained and rinsed
salt and black pepper

BUTTER BEAN PURÉE
1 x 400-g/14-oz. can butter beans, drained and rinsed
2 tbsp lemon juice
½ tsp salt
handful of coriander/cilantro leaves

BLACK GARLIC DRESSING
5 black garlic cloves
1½ tbsp balsamic vinegar
1½ tbsp soy sauce
1 tbsp olive oil

SERVES 4–6

Preheat the oven to 220°C/200°C fan/425°F/Gas 7. Toss the squash with 2 tablespoons of the oil and spread out over your largest roasting tray. Season with salt and roast for 10 minutes.

Meanwhile, make the butter bean purée. In a blender or food processor, whizz together all the beans, lemon juice and salt with 2–3 tablespoons water to a soft, smooth purée. Briefly blend in the coriander, then spread over the base of a large serving platter.

Stir the chicory and shallots into the tray with the squash, drizzle with another 1 tablespoon of the oil and roast for 10 minutes.

Meanwhile, make the black garlic dressing. In a bowl, mash the black garlic cloves with the back of a fork. Stir in the remaining ingredients until combined.

Stir the butter beans into the roasting tray with the vegetables. Drizzle with a final tablespoon of oil and season with salt and pepper. Roast for a final 10 minutes.

To serve, pile the roasted vegetables and beans over the butter bean purée. Spoon over the dressing and serve immediately.

COOK'S TIP *Black garlic is aged and slowly heated garlic. It has a mellow, tangy flavour and goes really well with balsamic vinegar. You can buy it from most major supermarkets now.*

PULSE SWAP *Use cannellini instead of butter beans.*

This is a great example of how pulses can be used to bulk up minced/ground meat – you can add crushed chickpeas/garbanzo beans to burgers, meatballs or the kofte here. It's a clever way to reduce meal costs while also boosting the nutritional profile of recipes.

LAMB & CHICKPEA KOFTES
with feta & mint

2 tbsp olive oil
1 onion, finely diced
2 garlic cloves, crushed
   or finely grated
1 tsp ground cumin
1 tsp ground turmeric
1 x 400-g/14-oz. can chickpeas/
   garbanzo beans, drained
   and rinsed
2 x 400-g/14-oz. cans chopped
   tomatoes
200 g/7 oz. feta cheese, broken
   into chunks
handful of mint and/or flat-leaf
   parsley leaves, shredded

LAMB KOFTE
1 x 400-g/14-oz. can chickpeas/
   garbanzo beans, drained
   and rinsed
500 g/1 lb. 2 oz. minced/
   ground lamb
1 small red onion, coarsely
   grated
2 garlic cloves, crushed
   or finely grated
1 tsp salt
2 tsp ras el hanout spice mix
   (see cook's tip)
black pepper

SERVES 6

Start by making the kofte. Use a fork or potato masher to crush the chickpeas in a large mixing bowl. Add the remaining ingredients and a good grind of black pepper and divide into 12 equal balls, then shape into torpedoes.

Heat the oil in a large sauté pan or shallow casserole over a medium-high heat. Add the kofte and fry, turning regularly, until golden all over, about 8–10 minutes. Lift out of the pan and set aside on a plate.

Add the onion and garlic to the pan with a good pinch of salt and fry for 6–8 minutes until soft and turning golden. Add the spices and fry for a minute more, then add the chickpeas and tomatoes. Bring to a gentle simmer, then nestle the koftes into the sauce. Simmer gently for 20 minutes. Taste the sauce, adding salt, pepper and a pinch of sugar as needed.

(You can now set aside the dish for up to 48 hours. Chill and when ready to serve, reheat the koftes and sauce in the pan – you may need to add a splash of water to loosen.)

Preheat the grill/broiler to high. Scatter over the feta and place under the grill for 5 minutes, or until soft and golden in places. Scatter with herbs and serve with couscous or bulgur wheat.

COOK'S TIP *Ras el hanout is a North African spice mix that goes really well with lamb. You can swap it for 1 teaspoon ground cumin and 1 teaspoon ground coriander.*

Fennel's anise crunch goes so well with soft butter beans and creamy burrata. Try to use the fresh juice squeezed from an orange for this salad, rather than from a carton.

BURRATA, BUTTER BEAN & FENNEL SALAD

1 ball burrata
2 tbsp extra virgin olive oil, plus extra to serve
1 tbsp lemon juice
1 tbsp orange juice (ideally squeezed from an orange), plus extra to serve
½ tsp runny honey
a small grating of garlic, no more than ¼ clove (optional)
1 fennel bulb
1 x 400-g/14-oz. can butter/lima beans, drained and rinsed
½ red onion, thinly sliced
2 tbsp roughly chopped dill
salt and black pepper

SERVES 2

Take the burrata out of the fridge 20–30 minutes before you want to serve it. It shouldn't be served fridge-cold.

In a mixing bowl, whisk together the oil, lemon and orange juices, honey and grated garlic (if using) with a pinch of salt and a grind of black pepper.

Trim the fronds from the fennel and set these aside. Cut the bulb in half lengthways, remove any tough or bruised outer leaves and cut out the tough core. Thinly slice the fennel and add to the citrus dressing with the beans, red onion and dill. Toss together and spread over a small platter.

Sit the burrata on top and gently break it open, drizzling it with a little more oil and seasoning with salt and pepper. Squeeze a little more orange juice over everything, scatter with the fennel fronds and serve immediately.

COOK'S TIP *This recipe can easily be doubled or tripled to serve more people.*

PULSE SWAP *Cannellini beans would also be great here.*

SOUPS & BROTHS

This is somewhere between a soup and a stew, and is completely moreish. The kind of thing I make for a light supper in summer when the weather isn't quite as warm as it should be.

BROTHY COURGETTE, BEANS & PASTA

3 tbsp olive oil
2 large courgettes/zucchini, trimmed and cut into 1-cm/½-inch dice
8 rashers smoked streaky/fatty bacon, roughly chopped
2 large leeks, trimmed, halved lengthways and thinly sliced
1 litre/4 cups chicken or veg stock
125 g/4½ oz. small pasta shapes (I like ditaloni)
2 x 400-g/14-oz. cans haricot/navy beans, drained and rinsed
a good squeeze of lemon juice
salt and black pepper
grated Parmesan, to serve

SERVES 2

Heat the oil in a large saucepan over a medium-high heat. Add the courgette and a good pinch of salt and fry, stirring regularly, for 8–10 minutes until golden all over. Scoop out of the pan (leaving the oil behind) and set aside.

Return the pan to the heat and fry the bacon for a couple of minutes. Add the leek and cook, stirring occasionally, for about 5 minutes. Add the chicken stock and the pasta and simmer for 2 minutes less than stated on the pasta packet.

Add the beans and simmer for a couple of minutes more, then taste to see if the pasta is fully cooked. Add the lemon juice, then season with a little more salt if needed. Spoon into bowls, scatter with the courgette and shower with grated Parmesan and a grind of black pepper.

COOK'S TIP *If you've cooked this in advance or are reheating leftovers, you may need to add a splash more water when warming it up, as the pasta will soak up the liquid as it cools.*

PULSE SWAP *This recipe works with any white beans, but I've used haricot because they are small and soft and almost melt into the broth.*

Pasta e ceci is a classic Italian dish of cucina povera ('poor kitchen' referring to the nation's tradition of peasant food). It makes a brilliant weeknight supper in the cooler months and can be on the table in less than 30 minutes. You can add a handful of chopped greens for the last couple of minutes of cooking, too.

PASTA & CHICKPEAS

3 tbsp olive oil
1 onion, finely diced
³/₄ tsp salt
3 garlic cloves, finely chopped
1 tbsp finely chopped rosemary
1 tbsp tomato purée/paste
1 x 400-g/14-oz. can chickpeas/
   garbanzo beans, drained
   and rinsed
1 litre/4 cups chicken or
   vegetable stock
1 Parmesan or pecorino rind
   (optional, see cook's tip)
150 g/5¹/₂ oz. short pasta
   shapes, like ditali or macaroni
grated Parmesan or pecorino,
   to serve (optional)

SERVES 4

Heat the oil in a large saucepan over a medium-high heat. Add the onion and salt and fry for 4–5 minutes until soft. Add the garlic and rosemary and fry for 1 minute. Stir in the tomato purée and fry, stirring, for a couple of minutes until slightly caramelized.

Stir in the chickpeas, stock and Parmesan rind (if using) and bring to a simmer. Add the pasta and simmer for 2 minutes less than the pack instructions.

Take off the heat and stand for a couple of minutes to allow the pasta to finish cooking. Serve with a grind of black pepper and some grated Parmesan or pecorino on top.

COOK'S TIP *Save your Parmesan (or pecorino) rinds for this soup as they add a lovely depth of flavour to the broth. You can pop them in the freezer until you need them and there's no need to defrost them before adding to the broth.*

Gazpacho is the perfect food for a sweltering day; light, refreshing and evoking memories of sun-drenched holidays in Spain. Traditionally the chilled soup is given its velvety body from white bread that has been soaked in water. White beans do a good job of replicating this, and I like to roast some extra beans with garlic to serve over the top.

GAZPACHO with
crunchy, garlicky beans

GAZPACHO
1/2 garlic clove, finely grated
500 g/1 lb. 2 oz. ripe tomatoes (5–6 medium tomatoes), roughly chopped
200 g/7 oz. cucumber (about 1/2 cucumber), roughly chopped
1/2 red (bell) pepper, deseeded and roughly chopped
1/2 x 400-g/14-oz. can haricot/navy beans, drained and rinsed
5 tbsp extra virgin olive oil
2 spring onions/scallions, roughly chopped
1 1/2–2 tbsp sherry vinegar
1/2–1 tsp sea salt
1/2 tsp caster/superfine sugar

TOPPING
1 x 400-g/14-oz. can haricot/navy beans, drained and rinsed
1 tbsp olive oil
1 1/2 garlic cloves, finely grated
1/2 tsp salt
200 g/7 oz. cucumber (about 1/2 cucumber), finely diced

SERVES 4

Put all the gazpacho ingredients into a high-speed blender with 100 ml/scant 1/2 cup cold water and whizz together. I like it smooth, although in many parts of Spain it is served with a slightly more grainy texture. Taste and add more vinegar and salt as desired. Add more cold water to achieve the right consistency if needed; thick but pourable. Chill for 1–2 hours.

Preheat the oven to 200°C/180°C fan/400°F/Gas 6.

For the topping, pat the beans dry with a paper towel. Toss with the oil, garlic and salt and spread over a roasting tray. Roast for 20 minutes, stirring halfway. Leave to cool (they'll hold for 1–2 hours before serving).

Serve the chilled soup in bowls or glasses and scatter with the crunchy beans and diced cucumber.

COOK'S TIP *You can easily halve or double this recipe to serve more or less.*

PULSE SWAP *A small white bean like cannellini or haricot is best used here.*

It is hard to express just how much I adore this soup. It is mellow, humble, deeply comforting and has seen me through many a winter. The cannellini beans not only thicken the soup but add a velvety, creamy texture. The kale crisps give good crunch, though you can serve without; it is a soup that can very much hold its own.

SMOKED HADDOCK, WHITE BEAN & CORN CHOWDER

about 240 g/8^{1}/$_{2}$ oz. smoked
   haddock
400 ml/1^{2}/$_{3}$ cups whole milk
30 g/2 tbsp unsalted butter
2 leeks, trimmed, halved
   lengthways and thinly sliced
1 large carrot, peeled, halved
   lengthways and thinly sliced
1 x 400-g/14-oz. can cannellini
   beans, drained and rinsed
200 g/1^{1}/$_{2}$ cups frozen or
   canned sweetcorn
500 ml/2 cups chicken or
   vegetable stock
juice of ^{1}/$_{2}$ lemon
salt and black pepper

CRISPY KALE
100 g/2^{1}/$_{2}$ cups kales leaves
   (no tough stalks), torn into
   small bite-size pieces
1 tbsp olive oil

SERVES 4

Place the haddock and milk in a medium saucepan. Set over a high heat until the milk is steaming hot with a few small bubbles on the surface. Take off the heat and set aside for 10 minutes. Lift the fish from the milk and set both aside separately.

Meanwhile, heat the butter in a large saucepan over a medium heat. Sweat the leeks and carrot with a large pinch of salt for 5–6 minutes until soft. Add the beans, corn and stock. Simmer for 5 minutes, then take off the heat and cool for 5 minutes.

For the kale crisps, preheat the oven to 160°C/140°C fan/320°F/ Gas 3. Toss the kale leaves and oil together and spread over a large parchment-lined baking tray. Season lightly with salt and bake for 12 minutes, or until crisp but still vibrant and green.

Transfer about two-thirds of the veg and stock to a blender. Add the lemon juice, a good grind of black pepper and the poaching milk. Whizz until smooth, then taste and season with more salt, pepper and lemon juice and whizz again. Return everything to the saucepan. Flake in the fish, discarding any skin.

Reheat the soup gently if necessary and serve scattered with the crispy kale.

COOK'S TIP *This soup will keep well in the fridge for 72 hours. It can also be frozen. When reheating, always do so gently, stirring regularly, and taking care not to boil it.*

PULSE SWAP *Any white beans will work well in this soup, try haricot/navy or butter/lima beans.*

*This is a stalwart winter soup for me.
It's sweet, earthy and herbaceous and
just makes you feel content.*

SWEET POTATO, ROSEMARY & LENTIL SOUP

500 g/1 lb. 2 oz. sweet potatoes, peeled and cut into 2.5-cm/1-inch cubes
3 tbsp olive oil
15 g/1 tbsp unsalted butter
100 g/3½ oz. cavolo nero, stalks thinly sliced and leaves shredded
1 leek, sliced
1 onion, diced
2 garlic cloves, crushed
3 rosemary sprigs, leaves finely chopped
½ tsp salt
250 g/1⅓ cups Puy/French, green or beluga lentils
1 litre/4 cups chicken or vegetable stock
juice of ½ lemon
salt and black pepper
grated Parmesan, to serve (optional)

SERVES 4

Preheat the oven to 220°C/200°C fan/425°F/Gas 8. Toss the sweet potato with 2 tablespoons of the oil, season and spread over a large non-stick baking tray. Roast for 25 minutes, stirring halfway, or until golden and soft.

Meanwhile, heat the remaining tablespoon of oil and the butter in a large saucepan over a medium-high heat. Fry the sliced cavolo nero stalks, leek, onion, garlic, rosemary and salt, stirring regularly, for 10 minutes. Add the lentils, shredded cavolo nero leaves and stock and bring to a simmer.

Take the roasted sweet potatoes out of oven and crush half of them with the back of a fork. Tip all of the potato into the pan and simmer for a final 5 minutes. Season to taste with lemon juice, salt and pepper. I like to serve this showered with grated Parmesan.

COOK'S TIP *Any greens would work in this recipe, use kale or spring greens instead of cavolo nero.*

PULSE SWAP *You could happily replace the lentils with chickpeas or cannellini beans. Black eyed beans/peas would be nice too.*

MISO SQUASH & ADUKI BEANS

3 heaped tbsp white miso paste
½ tsp mild chilli/chile powder
2 tbsp light soy sauce
3 garlic cloves, finely grated
1 tsp runny honey
600 ml/2½ cups boiling water
800 g/1¾ cups squash (ideally kabocha or butternut works well too), peeled, deseeded and cut into large chunks
1 x 400-g/14-oz. can aduki beans, drained and rinsed
1 tsp toasted sesame oil
4 spring onions/scallions, thinly sliced
toasted sesame seeds, to serve

SERVES 4

In a large saucepan, stir together the miso paste, chilli powder, soy, garlic and honey. Pour over the boiling water and add the squash. Bring to the boil, then lower to a simmer, cover with a lid and cook for 15–20 minutes, or until the squash is just tender.

Uncover and add the beans and simmer for another 6–7 minutes. Take off the heat and stir in the toasted sesame oil. Ladle into bowls and scatter with sliced spring onions and toasted sesame seeds to serve.

COOK'S TIP *Swap the honey for brown sugar or maple syrup for a vegan option.*

PULSE SWAP *You could happily swap the aduki beans for black or kidney beans. Due to their dark colour they are all good sources of anthocyanins (antioxidants).*

Pictured on page 113

Aduki (or adzuki) beans are small reddish-brown beans that are commonly eaten in Asia. They are often cooked, then puréed with sugar to make red bean paste to use in sweets and desserts. Here they are soft and mellow in this simple Japanese-inspired one pot that's brimming with flavour. Serve over rice or enjoy just as it is as a chunky soup

This is the kind of soup I could eat all day every day. It is like a golden elixir that warms the heart and feeds the soul. It is just as good without the meatballs, and can easily be entirely plant-based if you make it with vegetable stock and serve with a dairy-free yogurt.

PERSIAN-INSPIRED SPLIT YELLOW PEA & RICE SOUP with lamb meatballs

150 g/³/₄ cup split yellow peas
50 g/¹/₄ cup basmati rice
2 tbsp olive oil
2 large onions, halved and sliced
¹/₂ tsp salt
2 garlic cloves, crushed
1 tsp cumin seeds
¹/₂ tsp ground cinnamon
¹/₂ tsp ground turmeric
1 litre/4 cups chicken or vegetable stock
juice of ¹/₂–1 lemon

LAMB MEATBALLS
300 g/10¹/₂ oz. minced/ ground lamb
¹/₂ tsp salt
1 tsp ras el hanout spice (optional)
splash of olive oil
black pepper

TO SERVE
Greek yogurt
shredded mint leaves
pomegranate seeds

SERVES 4

Start by rinsing and soaking the split peas and rice (see cook's tip). Heat the oil in a large saucepan over a medium-high heat. Add the sliced onions and salt and fry for 10 minutes until soft. Add the garlic and fry for another 10 minutes until golden and caramelized. Scoop a spoonful of the onions out of the pan and set aside to use as a garnish.

Add the spices and fry for a minute, stirring constantly to make sure they don't catch. Add the stock, 500 ml/2 cups water and drained split peas and bring to a gentle simmer. Cook for 45 minutes, by which point the peas should be soft and breaking apart.

Meanwhile, make the meatballs. Preheat the oven to 180°C/160°C fan/350°F/Gas 4. Mix the lamb, salt and ras el hanout (if using) in a bowl with plenty of black pepper. Shape into 12 small meatballs and place in a roasting tin with a splash of oil. Roast for 15 minutes, shaking halfway, then set aside.

Drain the rice and add to the saucepan. Cover with a lid and simmer gently for 20 minutes, or until the rice is cooked (you may need to add a little more water during cooking). Add the juice of ¹/₂ lemon, then season to taste adding more salt, pepper and lemon juice as needed.

Tip the meatballs into the soup (leaving the fat in the roasting tin) and simmer for a final couple of minutes. Serve the soup topped with yogurt, shredded mint leaves, pomegranate seeds and the reserved onions.

COOK'S TIP *Rinse the split yellow peas and basmati rice in separate bowls. Place each in a mixing bowl, cover with cold water, then agitate the peas and rice grains with your hand. Pour off the cloudy water and repeat the process two more times or until the water is no longer cloudy. Leave to soak in cold water until ready to use.*

Bringing a Thai green curry vibe, this is a fabulous soup fragrant with lime leaves and lemongrass. If serving vegans, use vegetable stock and swap the fish sauce for soy sauce (or vegan fish sauce).

BROCCOLI, BUTTER BEAN & COCONUT SOUP

3 tbsp vegetable or sunflower oil
1 onion, diced
2 garlic cloves, crushed
4 fresh makrut lime leaves, stalks removed and leaves thinly sliced
2 lemongrass stalks, ends trimmed and thinly sliced
$1^1/_2$ tsp ground coriander
500 g/1 lb. 2 oz. broccoli (florets and stalks)
1 x 400-g/14-oz. can butter/ lima beans, drained and rinsed
500 ml/2 cups chicken or vegetable stock
1 x 400-ml/14-oz. can coconut milk
juice of $^1/_2$ lime, plus extra to taste
1 tbsp maple syrup, plus 1 tsp for the topping and extra to taste
$1^1/_2$ tbsp fish sauce, plus 1 tsp for the topping and extra to taste
salt

SERVES 4

Heat 2 tablespoons of the oil in a large saucepan over a medium-hight heat. Fry the onion, garlic and a pinch of salt for about 5–6 minutes. Add the lime leaves, lemongrass and ground coriander and cook for another 2 minutes.

Meanwhile, chop 150 g/5$^1/_2$ oz. small-medium florets from the broccoli and set aside for the topping. Roughly chop the remaining florets and stalks and add to the saucepan, frying for a minute.

Add half the beans, the stock and coconut milk to the pan and simmer gently for 5 minutes until the broccoli is just tender. Blend with the lime juice, 1 tablespoon maple syrup and 1$^1/_2$ tablespoons fish sauce. Taste, adding more lime, maple or fish sauce as desired.

Preheat the oven to 200°C/180°C fan/400°F/Gas 6. Toss the remaining butter beans with $^1/_2$ tablespoon oil and a good pinch of sea salt; spread over one side of a baking tray and roast for 10 minutes. Toss the reserved broccoli florets with the remaining $^1/_2$ tablespoon oil, 1 teaspoon maple syrup and 1 teaspoon fish sauce. Add to the other side of the tray and roast everything for a final 10 minutes.

Reheat the soup if necessary and divide among bowls. Scatter with the roasted broccoli and butter beans and serve immediately. Any leftover soup will freeze well.

COOK'S TIP *Try to get fresh makrut lime leaves for this as they have much more flavour than dried. They are available in most major supermarkets now, and they freeze well so you can keep a stash for when you need them.*

I consider myself a bit of a chicken soup connoisseur. I've been making my mother's Jewish chicken soup for decades and along the way I've flirted with different methods. Roasting the chicken and veg before simmering means you end up with a flavoursome, darker broth. Here the broth is turned into my version of caldo de pollo, a veg-packed chicken soup.

MEXICAN-STYLE CHICKEN & BLACK BEAN SOUP

ROASTED CHICKEN BROTH
800 g/1³/₄ lb. chicken drumsticks
2 onions, unpeeled and halved
2 carrots, unpeeled and halved
3 garlic cloves, unpeeled
2 jalapeño chillies/chiles
2 bay leaves
8 black peppercorns
handful of coriander/cilantro
  stalks
1 tsp salt

TO FINISH
1 tbsp neutral cooking oil
2 carrots, peeled and thinly
  sliced into rounds
1 large leek, trimmed, halved
  lengthways and chopped
2 sweetcorn cobs, halved
1 x 400-g/14-oz. can black
  beans, drained and rinsed
2 limes, halved
1 jalapeño chilli/chile, thinly
  sliced
handful of coriander/
  cilantro leaves

SERVES 4

Preheat the oven to 200°C/180°C fan/400°F/Gas 6. Spread the chicken, onions, carrots, garlic and chillies out in a roasting tin. Roast for 25–30 minutes.

Tip the roasted chicken and veg into a large pot. Add any roasting juices and add a splash of just-boiled water to the tin to scrape out any caramelized bits – these have lots of flavour.

Add 3 litres/quarts water, the bay, peppercorns, coriander stalks and salt, bring to a simmer and then lower the heat so there are just a few gentle bubbles rising to the surface. Cook like this for 2¹/₂ hours, skimming any scum from the surface as it appears. Take off the heat and cool for 30 minutes.

Drain the broth through a fine sieve/strainer into a large jug/pitcher or bowl, pressing the vegetables to extract as much liquid as possible. Shred the meat from the chicken, discarding the skin and bones, and add to the broth. Discard everything else.

Heat the oil in a large saucepan over a medium heat. Fry the carrots and leeks with a pinch of salt for about 5 minutes until softened. Add the broth and chicken meat to the pan, along with the sweetcorn and black beans. Simmer everything gently for 10 minutes. Taste the broth and add more salt if needed. Ladle into bowls, adding half a lime to each (to be squeezed in before eating), some sliced jalapeño and a few coriander leaves.

COOK'S TIP *The lime juice will turn the broth cloudy, so allow everyone to squeeze in their own just before eating.*

PULSE SWAP *Try black eyed beans/peas or cannellini beans.*

PURE
COMFORT

This is rustic, farmhouse cooking with a distinctly Gallic accent. It is humble and heart-warming, and can be simply served as it is or with some garlic mayonnaise, crusty bread and a crisp green salad with a mustardy dressing.

BRAISED CHICKEN & FLAGEOLET

4 chicken thighs
  (skin-on and bone-in)
2 fennel bulbs
1 tbsp olive oil
150 g/5½ oz. smoked bacon
  lardons
1 echalion/banana shallot or
  small onion, halved and sliced
  lengthways
2 garlic cloves, sliced
150 ml/⅔ cup white wine
250 ml/1 cup chicken stock
1 x 400-g/14-oz. can flageolet
  beans, drained and rinsed
salt

SERVES 4

Take the chicken out of the fridge 30 minutes before you wish to cook it. Season all over with salt and set aside.

Meanwhile, prepare the fennel. Trim the fronds and set aside to garnish. Trim the base, then cut out and discard the hard core. Remove any thick or tough outer layers and slice thinly. Cut the remaining fennel into chunky slices; set aside.

Preheat the oven to 180°C/160°C fan/350°F/Gas 4. Heat the oil in a large ovenproof sauté pan or shallow casserole over a medium-high heat. Pat the chicken dry, then add to the hot oil, skin-side down. Fry for 6–8 minutes, or until golden, then turn and fry on the flesh side for 2 minutes. Remove from the pan and set aside.

Add the lardons (there should be plenty of fat left in the pan) and fry for 5 minutes, then add the fennel, shallot and garlic with a pinch of salt. Fry for another 6–8 minutes until the vegetables are starting to soften.

Add the wine to the pan and bubble until reduced by half, then add the stock. Bring to a simmer and nestle the chicken back into the pan skin-side up. Transfer to the oven and cook for 20 minutes.

Stir the beans into the pan (you may want to lift the chicken out for a minute while you do this), then return to the oven for about 15–20 minutes, or until the chicken is cooked through and the juices run clear when pierced with a skewer. Stand for 5 minutes before serving.

COOK'S TIP *If I ever have any leftover wine in a bottle, I weigh it and freeze it labelling the container with the amount. It can come in very handy for recipes like this.*

PULSE SWAP *Any small bean would work here – try cannellini or haricot/navy.*

The key to the success of this recipe is the browning of the aubergine/eggplant and onions. They should be golden and caramelized to give this dish its full flavour, so it's worth taking your time over cooking them. Wonderful served over pasta, with gnocchi or polenta, or simply with crusty bread to scoop it up.

CARAMELIZED AUBERGINE & LENTIL RAGÙ

3 tbsp olive oil
2 aubergines/eggplants, trimmed and cut into 2-cm/³/₄-inch cubes
2 onions, diced
2 garlic cloves, finely chopped
1 heaped tbsp tomato purée/paste
1 tsp paprika
¹/₂ tsp ground allspice
1 cinnamon stick (optional)
2 bay leaves
250 g/9 oz. cooked brown, Puy/French or Beluga lentils
1 x 400-g/14-oz. can chopped tomatoes
4 fresh oregano sprigs (optional)
salt
basil, to garnish
pasta, polenta or bread, to serve

SERVES 4

Heat the oil in a large sauté pan or shallow casserole over a medium-high heat. Add the aubergines, onions and garlic, sprinkle generously with salt and cover with a lid. Cook, stirring occasionally, for 15 minutes.

The aubergines should be nicely softened by now, so remove the lid and continue cooking for another 15 minutes until everything is nicely golden and starting to caramelize.

Stir in the tomato purée, spices and bay leaves and fry for about 2 minutes. Finally, stir in the lentils, tomatoes and oregano sprigs (if using). Half fill the tomato can with water and also add to the pan. Simmer for 15–20 minutes until you have a rich ragù.

Season to taste and serve garnished with basil, with pasta, polenta or bread.

COOK'S TIP *This recipe freezes really well. Divide into portions of 200 g/7 oz. per person.*

This is inspired by a classic Jamaican oxtail and butter bean stew, which is traditionally made with whole allspice berries and Scotch bonnet chilli/chile. It's everything an oxtail stew should be – rich, deep and full-bodied. You can use beef cheeks or shin as an alternative to oxtail, and serve with rice, polenta or couscous.

SPICED OXTAIL & BUTTER BEANS

1.5 kg/3¼ lb. oxtail, in 5-cm/2-inch chunks
2 tbsp olive or vegetable oil
1 large onion, diced
2 carrots, roughly chopped
3 garlic cloves, crushed
1 heaped tsp grated fresh root ginger
1 green chilli/chile, whole but pierced 3–4 times with a knife
2 tbsp tomato purée/paste
1 tsp smoked paprika
1 tsp ground allspice
1 tsp ground coriander
500 ml/2 cups chicken or beef stock
1½ tbsp Worcestershire sauce
2 x 400-g/14-oz. cans butter/lima beans, drained and rinsed
salt and black pepper

SERVES 4–6

Take the oxtail out of the fridge at least 30 minutes before you plan to cook it. Season it all over with salt and set aside.

Preheat the oven to 160°C/140°C fan/320°F/Gas 3. Heat the oil in a large casserole or ovenproof sauté pan over a high heat. Pat the oxtail dry with paper towels and fry, turning regularly, for about 12 minutes until well browned all over. Remove from the pan and set aside.

Turn the heat under the pan to medium-high. You want about 2 tablespoons of the oil in the pan, so either scoop some out or add a splash more if needed. Fry the onion and carrots with a pinch of salt for about 5 minutes until starting to soften. Add the garlic, ginger and chilli and fry for 2 minutes. Next add the tomato purée and spices and fry for another 2 minutes until the purée has darkened and caramelized.

Return the oxtail to the pan with any resting juices. Add the stock, 500 ml/2 cups water and the Worcestershire sauce. Season with a little salt and plenty of ground black pepper. Cover with a tight-fitting lid and transfer to the oven. Cook for 1½ hours, stirring it halfway and turning the meat.

Uncover the pan and cook for 45 minutes. Stir in the butter beans and turn the meat and cook for a final 45 minutes. By the end of cooking the meat should be falling off the bones and the sauce thick and glossy. If not, return to the oven, checking it every 15 minutes. Stand for 10 minutes before serving.

COOK'S TIP *Like most slow-cooked stews, this tastes better made a day in advance and reheated to serve. It also freezes well, in which case it's best to pull the meat from the bones beforehand.*

PULSE SWAP *This is best with butter beans, but you could use any beans really. Chickpeas/garbanzo beans would also work well.*

MOONG DAL TADKA

200 g/1 cup moong dal
1 tbsp neutral cooking oil
1 small onion, diced
**15 g/^{1}/$_2$ oz. fresh root ginger,
   peeled and finely chopped**
1 tomato, chopped
1 tsp garam masala
^{1}/$_2$ tsp ground turmeric
^{1}/$_4$ tsp mild chilli/chile powder
1 tsp salt
juice of ^{1}/$_2$ lemon

TADKA
2 tbsp neutral cooking oil
^{1}/$_2$ tsp cumin seeds
^{1}/$_2$ tsp black mustard seeds
1 dried red chilli/chile
4 garlic cloves, finely sliced
8 curry leaves

SERVES 4

Place the dal in a mixing bowl and cover with cold water, then agitate with your hands. Pour off the cloudy water and repeat the process two more times, or until the water is no longer cloudy. Set aside to soak in cold water.

Meanwhile, heat the oil in a large saucepan over a medium-high heat. Fry the onion for 3–4 minutes, then add the ginger and tomato and fry for a couple of minutes more. Add the garam masala, turmeric and chilli powder and fry for a minute more.

Add the drained dal, 800 ml/3^1/$_4$ cups water and the salt and bring to the boil, then lower to a simmer and cook, stirring occasionally, for 30–45 minutes, or until the lentils are completely soft. Take off the heat.

For the tadka, heat the oil in a small frying pan/skillet over a high heat. Add the cumin and mustard seeds and fry briefly until they start to splutter. Add the dried chilli and garlic and fry until the garlic starts to turn golden. Finally add the curry leaves and cook for another 30 seconds.

Tip the tadka into the saucepan of hot dal and cover with a lid to keep all the aromas in. Leave to stand for 10 minutes, then stir together with the lemon juice. Season with more salt if needed and serve with steamed basmati rice.

COOK'S TIP *This dal freezes very well. I like to pack it into 200-g/7-oz. portions and freeze them individually.*

Delicate flageolet beans bring a lightness to this robust stew, while the spices have a mulled wine vibe adding depth and verve.

LAMB, RED WINE & FLAGEOLET BEANS

750 g/1 lb. 10 oz. lamb
   neck fillet, cut into
   large chunks
2 tbsp olive oil
2 onions, halved
   and sliced
2 carrots, peeled
   and diced
4 garlic cloves,
   finely chopped
2 cinnamon sticks
3 cloves
1 bay leaf
1/2 tsp ground allspice

250 ml/1 cup red wine
1 x 400-g/14-oz. can
   chopped tomatoes
250 ml/1 cup chicken,
   lamb or veg stock
a pinch of sugar
2 x 400-g/14-oz. cans
   flageolet beans,
   drained and rinsed
salt and black pepper
chopped flat-leaf
   parsley, to garnish

SERVES 6

Take the lamb out of the fridge at least 30 minutes before you want to cook it. Season all over with salt and pepper and set aside until ready to cook.

Heat the oil in a large casserole over a high heat. Brown the lamb on all sides for about 8 minutes. Scoop out of the pan and set aside on a plate. Lower the heat to medium-high and fry the onions, carrots and garlic with a pinch of salt for about 10 minutes until soft and turning golden.

Add the spices to the pan and fry for a minute, then add the wine and bubble until reduced by half. Return the meat to the pan along with the tomatoes, stock, a pinch of sugar and a good grind of black pepper. Bring to a gentle simmer, cover with a tight-fitting lid and cook for 1 hour, stirring halfway.

Uncover the pan, stir in the beans and simmer gently without a lid for a final hour, stirring from time to time. The stew is ready when the meat is tender and the sauce is rich and glossy. Scatter with chopped parsley and serve with mashed potato, couscous or orzo.

BUTTER BEAN & ROOT VEG GRATIN

750 g/1 lb. 10 oz.
   mixed root veg (such
   as celeriac, parsnip
   and sweet potato)
1 tbsp olive oil
1 tbsp unsalted butter
1 onion, thinly sliced
1 tsp salt
1 leek, thinly sliced
2 garlic cloves, thinly
   sliced
300 ml/1 1/4 cups
   double/heavy cream
175 ml/3/4 cup full-fat/
   whole milk

2 tsp Dijon mustard
2 x 400-g/14-oz. cans
   butter/lima beans,
   drained and rinsed
5 thyme sprigs,
   leaves stripped
a grating of nutmeg
120 g/4 1/2 oz. mature
   Cheddar cheese,
   coarsely grated
40 g/1 1/2 oz. panko
   breadcrumbs

SERVES 4–6

Preheat the oven to 200°C/180°C fan/400°F/Gas 6. Peel the root veg and slice it as thinly as you can using a sharp chef's knife or mandoline.

Heat the oil and butter in a large sauté pan or shallow casserole over a medium-high heat. Fry the onion and 1/2 teaspoon of the salt for 5 minutes until starting to soften. Add the leek and garlic and fry for another 3–4 minutes.

Tip all the root veg into the pan along with the remaining salt and cook, stirring over the heat, for another 6–8 minutes until the vegetables are starting to soften. Add the cream, milk, mustard and beans, most of the thyme and a generous grating of nutmeg. Stir together and bring to a gentle simmer. Cook for 2–3 minutes, then add two-thirds of the cheese and stir while it melts. Taste and season with salt and pepper.

Transfer to a 1.5-litre/quart baking dish. Mix the remaining cheese, thyme and the breadcrumbs and sprinkle over the top. Bake for 25–30 minutes until golden. Stand for 5 minutes before serving.

Pictured on page 133

This butter bean and veg gratin is rich, warming and guaranteed to make anyone who eats it very happy. Serve as a main with a green salad or as a side to roast chicken or lamb.

I feel like mung beans get a bad rap, associated with being an overly virtuous health food. They are certainly virtuous – packed with minerals and antioxidants – which is no bad thing, but they taste wonderful too, so do set aside any preconceived ideas. They cook down to a soft and creamy texture and are delicious in this spiced coconutty stew. Incidentally, the beansprouts we are accustomed to eating are sprouted from mung beans.

COCONUT MUNG BEANS
with garlicky green beans

200 g/1 cup mung beans
2 tbsp cooking oil
   (such as vegetable or olive)
1 onion, finely diced
2 garlic cloves, finely chopped
20 g/³/₄ oz. fresh root ginger,
   finely grated
1 tsp salt
1 tsp garam masala
1 tsp ground cumin
¹/₂ tsp ground turmeric
¹/₂ tsp mild chilli/chile powder
1 x 400-g/14-oz. can chopped
   tomatoes
1 x 400-g/14-oz. can coconut
   milk
juice of ¹/₂ lime
salt and black pepper
flatbreads, to serve

GARLICKY GREEN BEANS
2 tbsp cooking oil
200 g/7 oz. fine green beans,
   trimmed and cut into
   4-cm/1¹/₂-inch lengths
2 garlic cloves, thinly sliced
1 tsp black mustard seeds

SERVES 4

Soak the mung beans in a bowl of cold water for at least 5 hours, or overnight.

Heat the oil in a large saucepan over a medium-high heat. Add the onion, garlic and ginger with ¹/₂ teaspoon salt and fry for 8 minutes, stirring regularly. Add the spices and fry for a minute more, then add the chopped tomatoes, coconut milk and 600 ml/2¹/₂ cups water (a good way to measure this is to fill the empty tomato can with water 1¹/₂ times to get any residual tomatoes out too).

Drain the mung beans and add to the pan with the remaining salt and a good grind of black pepper. Simmer for 35–40 minutes or until the mung beans are soft and start to break apart. Squeeze in the lime juice. You may need to add a splash more water too.

For the garlicky beans, heat the oil in a frying pan/skillet over a medium-high heat. Add the beans and fry for a minute, then add the garlic and a pinch of salt and fry for another 1–2 minutes, or until the garlic is turning golden. Add the mustard seeds and fry, stirring regularly, until the seeds pop, the garlic is deep golden and the beans are soft. Serve scattered over the mung beans, with some flatbreads on the side too, if you like.

COOK'S TIP *The mung beans taste better if made a day in advance. This dish also freezes well too.*

PULSE SWAP *You could also make this recipe with red lentils, although they don't need soaking in advance.*

I love pot-roasting chicken as you end up with perfectly tender meat (especially the breast) and a flavour-packed sauce full of the chicken-y juices. This is a gorgeous meal to serve on an autumnal/fall day, alongside a green salad and some crusty bread to mop up the sauce.

POT-ROAST CHICKEN
with borlotti & rosemary

1.5-kg/3¼-lb. whole chicken (ideally free-range)
2 tbsp olive oil
4 bushy rosemary sprigs
1 garlic bulb, halved
½ lemon
2 large onions, halved and sliced
250 ml/1 cup chicken stock
125 ml/½ cup white wine
2 x 400-g/14-oz. cans borlotti/cranberry beans, drained and rinsed
5 tbsp double/heavy cream
salt

SERVES 4–6

Take the chicken out of the fridge at least 30 minutes before you plan to cook it. Remove all packaging and season inside and out with salt; set aside until ready to cook.

Heat the oil in a large casserole over a medium-high heat. Add the chicken and brown on all sides, turning it regularly. Lift out of the pan and onto a plate. Stuff the cavity with 1 rosemary sprig, half the garlic bulb and the lemon half.

Lower the heat under the casserole to medium and add the onions, remaining half of the garlic bulb and a good pinch of salt. Fry for 6–8 minutes until the onions are soft and turning golden. Chop the leaves from 2 of the rosemary sprigs and add to the pan, frying for a minute more.

Nestle the chicken back into the pan. Add the stock and wine, bring to the boil, then turn the heat to low. Cover the casserole with a lid and cook for 1 hour.

Take off the lid and lift the chicken onto a plate to rest for about 10 minutes. Meanwhile, add the borlotti beans, cream and remaining whole rosemary sprig to the casserole and simmer for a final 10 minutes. Taste the sauce and season as needed, then carve the chicken and serve together. You can squeeze the soft cloves from the garlic bulb into the sauce too, if you like.

COOK'S TIP *The one thing you miss with pot-roasting chicken is the crispy skin, but it's still worth taking your time to brown it first so you get all the flavour.*

PULSE SWAP *Any white beans would be wonderful in this recipe: try cannellini, flageolet or butter/lima beans.*

It would be remiss to write a cookbook on pulses without a recipe for beef chilli/chili with kidney beans. You could swap the beef short ribs for 400 g/14 oz. braising beef cut into chunks and reduce the oven time.

ANCHO CHILLI SHORT RIBS, KIDNEY BEANS & SQUASH

1.5 kg/3¼ lb. short ribs
500 g/1 lb. 2 oz. butternut
  squash, peeled,
  deseeded and cut into
  1-cm/½-inch slices
2 tbsp olive oil
1 large red onion, diced
3 garlic cloves, crushed
1 heaped tbsp tomato
  purée/paste
1 heaped tbsp ancho chilli/
  chile flakes, plus extra
  to serve (see cook's tip)
1 tsp ground cumin
½ tsp ground cinnamon
1 x 400-g/14-oz. can
  chopped tomatoes
500 ml/2 cups beef
  (or chicken) stock
zest and juice of 1 orange
2 x 400-g/14-oz. cans red
  kidney beans, drained
  and rinsed
juice of 1 lime
salt and black pepper
rice and soured cream,
  to serve

PICKLED RED ONIONS
1 small red onion, halved
  and thinly sliced
2 tbsp cider vinegar
2 tsp runny honey
½ tsp fine salt

SERVES 4–6

Take the short ribs out of the fridge 30 minutes before you want to cook them. Season with salt and pepper and set aside at room temperature.

Mix the pickled red onion ingredients in a bowl and set aside.

Preheat the oven to 220°C/200°C fan/425°F/Gas 7. Toss the squash with 1 tablespoon of the oil, season and spread out on a baking tray. Roast for 20 minutes, stirring halfway, then set aside.

Meanwhile, heat the remaining oil in a large lidded casserole or sauté pan over a medium-high heat. Fry the short ribs, browning on all sides, for 8–10 minutes. Lift out of the pan and set aside. Spoon out any excess fat from the pan (you want 1–2 tablespoons in there) and fry the onion and garlic for 6–8 minutes until starting to soften and turn golden. Stir in the tomato purée and spices and fry for a minute more.

Add the tomatoes, stock, orange zest and juice to the pan, then return the short ribs along with any resting juices. Add a good pinch of salt and plenty of black pepper and cover with a lid. Place in the oven, lower the heat to 160°C/140°C fan/425°F/Gas 3 and cook for 1¾ hours, turning the ribs every 35 minutes if not fully submerged in the liquid.

Take the pan out of the oven, uncover and spoon off any excess fat that sits on top. Stir in the kidney beans and roasted squash and cook, uncovered, for another hour, or until the meat is falling off the bone and the sauce glossy and thick. Leave to stand for 10 minutes, then stir in the lime juice. Serve with the pickled onions, soured cream, rice and an extra pinch of chilli flakes if you like.

COOK'S TIP *Ancho chillies are a mild and fruity dried Mexican chillies with a warming backheat. You can buy them in flakes or ground from major supermarkets or online (Mexgrocer.co.uk). Alternatively you could use 1 teaspoon chipotle chilli paste or powder, or mild chilli powder.*

This is crowd-pleasing comfort food at its best. Using the bean liquid helps make a creamy sauce, so make sure you buy a good-quality option (see page 10).

CHICKEN, MUSHROOM & BUTTER BEAN PIE

1 tbsp unsalted butter

2 tbsp olive oil

250 g/9 oz. chestnut mushrooms, cleaned, trimmed and quartered

500 g/1 lb. 2 oz. skinless, boneless chicken thighs, cut into bite-size pieces

2 leeks, trimmed, halved lengthways and roughly chopped

3 thyme sprigs, leaves stripped

100 ml/scant 1/2 cup chicken stock

1 x 400-g/14-oz. can butter/lima beans, drained (reserving the liquid, see below) and rinsed

100–150 ml/1/2–2/3 cup bean liquid

2 tsp wholegrain mustard

3 tbsp double/heavy cream

320 g/11 1/2 oz. all-butter puff pastry sheet

1 egg, lightly beaten for glazing

salt and black pepper

1–1.5-litre/quart pie dish

SERVES 4–6

Heat the butter and 1 tablespoon of the oil in a large frying pan/skillet over a high heat. Add the mushrooms, a good pinch of salt and a grind of black pepper. Fry for about 8 minutes, or until golden; tip into a bowl and set aside.

Add the remaining 1 tablespoon oil to the pan and fry the chicken with a pinch of salt for 5–6 minutes until golden in places. Add the leeks, lower the heat to medium-high and cook, stirring regularly, for another 5–6 minutes.

Add the thyme, chicken stock, beans and their liquid and simmer everything together for about 5 minutes, or until coated in a thick sauce. Stir in the mustard and double cream and simmer for a final minute. Taste to check the seasoning, then take off the heat and set aside to cool for 30 minutes.

Preheat the oven to 200°C/180°C fan/400°F/Gas 6. Stir the mushrooms through the mixture and tip into the pie dish. Top with the puff pastry and trim the edges.

Cut a small cross in the middle to let the steam escape, then score the pastry in a circular pattern, radiating from the centre out toward the edges. Brush beaten egg over the pastry and bake for about 30 minutes or until golden.

COOK'S TIP *You can assemble the pie up to 48 hours in advance and bake to serve.*

PULSE SWAP *Any white beans like cannellini, flageolet or haricot/navy would be nice in the pie filling.*

DIPS,
SIDES &
SNACKS

We're all a little fixated on how good houmous is (which is fair enough because it is), but white beans are also fabulous when blended to a dip. For maximum energy efficiency, add the leeks to the oven while something else is cooking.

WHITE BEAN DIP
with sweet leeks & capers

2 large leeks (about 400 g/
   14 oz.), rinsed of any dirt
2 large garlic cloves
1 x 400-g/14-oz. can haricot/
   navy beans, drained
   and rinsed
3 tbsp olive oil (use extra
   virgin if you have it)
1 tbsp lemon juice
½ tsp salt
1 tbsp small capers, such as
   nonpareille, chopped

SERVES 2–4

Preheat the oven to 200°C/180°C fan/400°F/Gas 6. Place the whole leeks and the garlic cloves on a roasting tray. Roast for 45 minutes, turning the leeks halfway through; set aside to cool for 15 minutes.

Place the beans in a blender (a high-speed one like a Nutribullet is perfect) with 2 tablespoons of the oil, the lemon juice and salt. Peel the garlic and add the soft flesh to the blender. Peel one of the leeks, removing and discarding the charred outer layer (and any other burnt bits). Chop the flesh and add to the blender. Whizz to a smooth purée then tip onto a plate or bowl.

Peel the remaining leek and finely chop the flesh. Stir together with the capers, the remaining 1 tablespoon oil and a pinch of salt. Spoon over the purée and serve immediately.

COOK'S TIP *You can make this dip up to 48 hours in advance. As well as serving as a dip, it goes really nicely as a side to steak.*

PULSE SWAP *Use any white beans – cannellini, butter/lima or haricot/navy work well.*

Confusingly this is not made from fava beans (which are a variety of broad bean), but from split yellow peas. The Greek island of Santorini, where this is commonly served, grows split yellow peas that are particularly prized due to its rich volcanic soil. Try serving it instead of houmous, your guests will love it.

GREEK-STYLE FAVA
with dill & feta

200 g/1 cup split yellow peas, well rinsed
5 tbsp olive oil (ideally extra virgin), plus a splash more to serve
2 onions, halved and sliced
1 tsp sea salt
2 garlic cloves, sliced
juice of 1/2 lemon, plus extra to taste

TO SERVE
75 g/2³/4 oz. feta, crumbled
3 tbsp chopped dill
toasted pitta bread
crudités

SERVES 4–6 AS A DIP

Place the rinsed split peas in a large saucepan and cover with plenty of cold water. Bring to the boil, then reduce to a brisk simmer and cook until completely softened and almost mushy (this usually takes 30–40 minutes). Top up the pan with water if needed during cooking.

Meanwhile, heat 3 tablespoons of oil in a large frying pan/skillet over a medium-high heat. Fry the onions and 1/2 teaspoon salt for 5 minutes, stirring regularly. Add the garlic and cook for another 15–20 minutes, or until deep golden and caramelized. They will need stirring more frequently towards the end of cooking and you may want to lower the heat a touch too. Scoop out a spoonful of the onions and garlic to use as a garnish, then set the pan aside off the heat.

Drain the peas, reserving the cooking liquor. Stir the peas into the pan with the onions and garlic, then transfer everything to a blender or food processor. Add the lemon juice, remaining salt, remaining oil and 6 tablespoons of the cooking liquor. Blend until smooth. Taste and season with more salt and lemon if desired. Tip into a bowl and cool to room temperature.

To serve, scatter with the reserved caramelized onions, crumbled feta and dill. Drizzle with a splash more oil and serve with toasted pitta bread and/or crudités.

COOK'S TIP *Fava tastes better if made ahead of eating, to allow the flavours to mingle. You can prepare it up to 48 hours in advance, chill it and then bring to room temperature before serving.*

I know how beloved baked beans on toast is in the UK, but this makes a very worthy alternative. The perfect late-night snack.

BEANS ON TOAST

2 tbsp olive oil
3 ripe tomatoes, halved
1 rosemary sprig
2 garlic cloves,
   unpeeled and bashed
1 x 400-g/14-oz. can
   flageolet beans,
   drained and rinsed
3 tbsp crème fraîche

2 thick slices of
   sourdough, toasted
   and buttered
salt and black pepper
grated Cheddar
   cheese, to serve
   (optional)

SERVES 2

Heat the oil in a medium frying pan/skillet over a medium heat. Season the cut side of the tomatoes, then add them, cut-side down, to the pan. Also add the rosemary and garlic cloves to the pan. Cook gently for 8–10 minutes until the tomatoes are nicely golden on top and starting to release their juices. Turn the tomatoes and cook for another 2–3 minutes.

Add the beans to the pan, stirring into the oil and tomato juices. Stir in the crème fraîche and heat for a minute, then season the beans to taste.

Arrange the buttered toast on plates and spoon over the tomatoes, beans and their sauce (discard the rosemary and garlic). Grate over a little Cheddar to serve, if liked.

COOK'S TIP *Add a splash of Worcestershire sauce to the beans if you have it.*

PULSE SWAP *Any beans would work here – try borlotti/cranberry, haricot/navy or cannellini.*

I was after a nut-free pesto to use in my daughter's lunchbox (as most schools are nut-free these days), and tried adding white beans instead of pine nuts. It's a brilliant swap, gives a nice creamy texture to the pesto and doesn't detract from the flavour. I usually add the leftover beans from the can to the hot pasta as I toss it with the pesto.

CANNELLINI BEAN PESTO

40 g/1¹/₂ oz. basil
1 x 400-g/14-oz. can
   cannellini beans,
   drained and rinsed
25 g/¹/₄ cup grated
   Parmesan
1 garlic clove,
   finely grated
zest of ¹/₂ lemon

90 ml/6 tablespoons
   extra virgin olive oil,
   plus extra to cover
salt and black pepper

MAKES ABOUT
200G/7 OZ.
(ROUGHLY
4 SERVINGS)

Place all of the ingredients in a small food processor with a good pinch of salt and a grind of black pepper. Whizz until smooth. Transfer to a small container and cover with a thin layer of extra oil (so that it doesn't discolour). Chill until ready to use.

COOK'S TIP *Add double the amount of beans to turn this into a summery dip to serve with crudité or to spread on bruschetta topped with chopped tomatoes.*

PULSE SWAP *Any white beans will work here, try butter/lima beans or haricot/navy.*

Pictured on page 151

Farinata is Italian street food, a thin pancake made from chickpea flour, which is cooked at a high heat to reveal crispy, lacy edges and an almost custardy centre. It is totally moreish and a fantastic gluten-free snack to serve at a party. I would also happily eat it for lunch with a tomato salad. In southern France it is known as 'socca'.

FARINATA

250 g/1²/₃ cups chickpea (gram) flour
650 ml/2³/₄ cups tepid water
1 tsp salt
4 tbsp olive oil
3 tbsp extra virgin olive oil
1 heaped tbsp chopped rosemary leaves
1 small red onion, thinly sliced
black pepper

MAKES 2 LARGE FARINATA

Place the chickpea flour in a mixing bowl and add the tepid warm and salt. Use a balloon whisk to whisk together. Don't worry if it's lumpy, it will hydrate as it rests. Set aside for 4–12 hours.

When ready to cook, preheat the oven to 240°C/220°C fan/460°F/ Gas 8 or to its highest setting. Place 2 tablespoons of the olive oil in a large ovenproof frying pan/skillet (ideally 30 cm/12 inches in diameter) and place in the oven to heat up for 10 minutes.

Whisk the extra virgin olive oil and rosemary into the batter, it should be completely smooth by now. Carefully remove the hot pan from the oven (keep a kitchen towel wrapped around the handle when it's out of the oven) and pour half of the batter in, swirling it so it reaches the edges of the pan. Scatter over half the onion and grind over some black pepper. Return to the oven for about 12 minutes until just turning golden on top.

Remove from the oven and then slide onto a chopping board, slice and serve. Cook the remaining batter in the same way, heating up the pan with the remaining 2 tablespoons olive oil again before adding the batter.

COOK'S TIP *Farinata is best eaten hot as it loses its crispness as it cools, although it's still very good at room temperature. You can also play around with the toppings; try adding some chopped sun-dried tomatoes or black olives.*

CHICKPEA, SPINACH & FETA PARCELS

500 g/10 cups fresh spinach
2 tbsp olive oil, plus 1–2 tbsp
    extra for brushing
1 onion, finely diced
150 g/3/4 cup cooked chickpeas/
    garbanzo beans
100 g/31/2 oz. feta cheese,
    crumbled
2 tsp za'atar, plus extra
    to sprinkle
4–5 sheets filo/phyllo pastry
salt and black pepper

MAKES 8–10

Place the spinach in a large bowl and pour over a kettle of just-boiled water. Press down with a wooden spoon to submerge the leaves and allow to wilt for a minute. Drain the spinach and rinse under cold water to cool, then squeeze between your hands in batches to remove as much water as possible. Pat dry thoroughly on paper towels and set aside until needed.

Heat 2 tablespoons oil in a large frying pan/skillet over a medium-high heat. Fry the onion with a pinch of salt for 5–6 minutes until just golden.

Meanwhile, roughly crush the chickpeas in a large bowl with a potato masher. Add them to the pan and fry for a minute more. Add the spinach and fry for 2 minutes; take off the heat and cool for 10 minutes.

Preheat the oven to 200°C/180°C fan/400°F/Gas 6. Line a large baking tray with baking parchment.

Halve the filo sheets lengthways to create long strips (about 10 cm/4 inches on the short side). Stir the feta and za'atar into the spinach mixture; taste and season with salt and pepper.

Take one filo strip and brush lightly all over with oil. Pile a generous spoonful of the mixture into the bottom corner. Fold the pastry strip up on the diagonal to create a triangular parcel encasing the filling. Don't wrap them too tightly or they'll split when they cook. Repeat using all the pastry and all the filling.

Place the parcels on the lined baking tray. Brush all over with more oil and scatter the tops with a little more zaatar. Bake for 20–25 minutes, or until golden and crisp. Cool for at least 10 minutes before serving. They are great warm or at room temperature.

COOK'S TIP *Blanching and wringing the spinach is an important step that shouldn't be missed. If skipped, the filling will be too wet as the spinach releases so much water as it cooks.*

These make a boldly flavoured snack,
or can be served as a main with a salad.
Use dairy-free yogurt if serving vegans.

CHICKPEA & CARROT FRITTERS
with curried yogurt dip

**2 x 400-g/14-oz. cans chickpeas/
garbanzo beans, drained
and rinsed**
1 large carrot, coarsely grated
1 small red onion, finely diced
1 heaped tsp cumin seeds
1 heaped tsp ground coriander
1 tsp salt
**bunch of fresh coriander/cilantro
(about 15 g/¹/₂ oz.), leaves
and stalks finely chopped**
5 tbsp chickpea (gram) flour
juice of 1 lime
**100 ml/scant ¹/₂ cup cooking oil
(vegetable or olive)**
200 g/7 oz. Greek yogurt
¹/₄ tsp mild curry powder
salt
lime wedges, to serve

SERVES 4

Place the chickpeas in a large mixing bowl and roughly crush with a potato masher or with the back of a fork. Add the carrot, onion, spices, salt, fresh coriander, chickpea flour and the juice of half the lime. Mix together with a spoon until combined.

It's worth making a test patty – shaping it and frying it in a little oil to see if it holds together. If It's a bit crumbly you might want to add a little extra chickpea flour and a splash of water to the mixture so it sticks together a bit more. Once you have the right consistency, shape into 10–12 patties.

Heat the oil in a large, non-stick frying pan/skillet over a medium-high heat. Fry in batches for 3–4 minutes on each side until golden. Remove from the pan and place on paper towels to soak up the excess oil.

While the fritters are cooking, mix the yogurt, curry powder, remaining juice of half the lime and a pinch of salt.

Serve the fritters with the yogurt dip and extra lime wedges for squeezing over.

COOK'S TIP *You can play around with the spices and veg in the fritters. Try any grated root vegetable instead of carrot, and use onion seeds instead of cumin.*

This is a very simple combination of ingredients inspired by the Italian flavours of cacio e pepe (cheese and pepper). I like to spoon it over a Caesar salad instead of croutons.

ROASTED CAULIFLOWER & BUTTER BEANS

1 medium cauliflower
  (about 1 kg/2¼ lb.)
2 tbsp olive oil
1 x 400-g/14-oz. can
  butter/lima beans,
  drained and rinsed

60 g/2 oz. pecorino
  cheese, finely grated
½ tsp ½ tsp coarsely
  ground black pepper

SERVES 4

Preheat the oven to 200°C/180°C fan/400°F/Gas 6.

Remove the cauliflower leaves and set any tender ones aside. Trim the thick core, then break or cut the cauliflower into medium florets. Toss with 1 tablespoon oil in a large roasting tin. Season very lightly with salt (remember the pecorino is salty) and roast for 10 minutes.

Meanwhile, pat the beans dry on paper towels. In a separate bowl, mix the cheese with the black pepper.

Toss the beans and the cauliflower leaves with the remaining tablespoon oil and add to the roasting tin. Scatter with two-thirds of the cheese and pepper mixture and toss everything together. Roast for 10 minutes.

Scatter over the remaining cheese and pepper and roast for a final 10–15 minutes until everything is golden and turning crisp in places. Cool for 5 minutes before serving.

I have always loved the flavour of Jamaican-style rice and peas (the peas usually being kidney beans). This is the perfect side to any grilled meat cooked in a jerk marinade.

RICE & PEAS

160-ml/5-oz. can
  coconut cream
300 ml/1¼ cups
  chicken (or
  vegetable) stock
4 spring onions/
  scallions, sliced
2 garlic cloves, crushed
5 allspice berries
  or ½ tsp ground
  allspice
4 thyme sprigs

¾ tsp salt
200 g/1¼ cups
  long-grain rice,
  well rinsed
1 x 400-g/14-oz. can
  red kidney beans,
  drained and rinsed
juice of 1 lime
black pepper

SERVES 4

Mix the coconut cream, stock, spring onions, garlic, allspice, thyme, salt and a good grind of black pepper in a medium-large saucepan. Set over a high heat.

As soon as it comes to the boil, add the rinsed and drained rice and kidney beans. Lower to a simmer and cook for 10 minutes.

Lower the heat to a very gentle simmer and cover with a lid. Cook like this for 5 minutes, then take the pan off the heat and stand, with the lid still on, for 10 minutes. Uncover, squeeze over the lime juice and fluff the rice with a fork.

SWEET THINGS

This is a wickedly good cake to feed a crowd with a soft, fudge-y crumb and a silky buttercream topping. You can top it with chocolate sprinkles, too.

FUDGE-Y BLACK BEAN CHOCOLATE SHEET CAKE

250 ml/1 cup sunflower or vegetable oil, plus extra for greasing
1 x 400-g/14-oz. can black beans, drained and rinsed
210 g/1½ cups plain/all-purpose flour
65 g/⅔ cup cocoa powder
300 g/1½ cups light brown soft sugar
2 tsp baking powder
1 tsp bicarbonate of soda/ baking soda
½ tsp fine salt
3 eggs
275 ml/1 cup plus 1½ tbsp just-boiled water
sprinkles, to decorate

CHOCOLATE ICING
100 g/3½ oz. dark/bittersweet chocolate (70% cocoa solids), chopped
125 g/½ cup plus 1 tbsp unsalted butter, softened
125 g/generous ¾ cup icing/ confectioners' sugar
1 tbsp cocoa powder
pinch of salt

33 x 22-cm/13 x 8¾-inch cake tin

SERVES 16

Preheat the oven to 180°C/160°C fan/350°F/Gas 4. Lightly grease the cake tin and line with baking parchment.

Whizz together the oil and beans in a blender until smooth.

In large mixing bowl, combine the flour, cocoa, sugar, baking powder, bicarbonate of soda and salt. In a jug/pitcher, lightly beat together the eggs with a fork.

Tip the blended oil and beans and the eggs into the mixing bowl with the dry ingredients. Stir together (don't worry if it's a bit dry), then pour over the just-boiled water. Use a balloon whisk to gently whisk together until smooth. Tip into the tin and bake for about 25 minutes, or until a skewer inserted into the centre comes out clean. Set aside to cool in the tin.

For the icing, melt the chocolate in a bowl, either in the microwave or over a saucepan of gently simmering water. Set aside to cool for 10 minutes.

Use electric beaters to whisk the butter for a minute until whippy. Sift in the icing sugar and cocoa and beat for another 2 minutes. Finally beat in the melted chocolate and a pinch of salt. Spread over the cake, decorate with sprinkles, then slice to serve.

COOK'S TIP *The cake will keep well in an airtight container for 3 days.*

The sesame topping is optional here, but it adds a gorgeously nutty, crunchy layer of flavour. Adding the beans means you need less fat and dairy in this recipe.

BEANY BANANA BREAD
with sesame crack topping

100 g/¹/₂ cup unsalted butter,
   plus extra for greasing
¹/₂ x 400-g/14-oz. can cannellini
   beans, drained and rinsed
2 eggs
1 tsp vanilla extract
250 g/9 oz. ripe banana
   (about 3 medium bananas)
175 g/1¹/₃ cups plain/all-purpose
   flour
1 tsp baking powder
¹/₂ tsp bicarbonate of soda/
   baking soda
¹/₂ tsp fine salt
125 g/²/₃ cup light brown
   soft sugar

**SESAME CRACK TOPPING
   (OPTIONAL)**
1 tbsp toasted white sesame
   seeds
1 tbsp caster/superfine sugar

900-g/2-lb. loaf tin

SERVES 10

Preheat the oven to 170°C/150°C fan/325°F/Gas 3. Grease and line the loaf tin with baking parchment.

Melt the butter in a medium saucepan, take off the heat and set aside to cool.

While the butter is cooling, whizz the beans, eggs and vanilla in a blender until smooth. Mash the bananas in a bowl with the back of a fork. Measure the flour, baking powder, bicarbonate of soda and salt into a bowl.

Mix together the sesame seeds and caster sugar for the topping, if using.

Using a balloon whisk, whisk the brown sugar into the pan with the butter. Next, whisk in the blended beans and eggs until combined, then whisk in the mashed banana. Finally, whisk in the flour, raising agents and salt until just combined.

Tip the mixture into the lined cake tin and evenly sprinkle over the sesame and sugar topping. Bake for 55–60 minutes, or until golden and a skewer inserted into the centre comes out clean. Cool completely in the tin before slicing to serve.

COOK'S TIP *To toast sesame seeds, place them in a frying pan/skillet over a medium heat. Shake from time to time (you'll need to do this more frequently the more colour they take on) until fragrant and golden. You can store any extra in a clean jar to sprinkle over soups, noodles and rice dishes.*

DOUBLE CHOCOLATE BROWNIE BEAN COOKIES

1 x 400-g/14-oz. can red kidney beans, drained and rinsed
75 g/¹/₃ cup unsalted butter, softened
75 g/¹/₃ cup caster/superfine sugar
50 g/1³/₄ oz. dark/bittersweet (70% cocoa solids) chocolate, melted
30 g/2 tbsp cocoa powder
1 tsp baking powder
1 egg
75 g/2³/₄ oz. white chocolate, cut into small chunks

MAKES 10

Place all of the ingredients, apart from the white chocolate chunks, in a food processor. Whizz until completely combined. Stir in the white chocolate chunks, scrape the mixture into a mixing bowl and chill for at least 2 hour (or up to 24 hours).

Preheat the oven to 180°C/160°C fan/350°F/Gas 4; line a large baking sheet with baking parchment.

Scoop spoonfuls of the cookie mixture and roll into balls. You should get 10 cookies from the mixture, each weighing about 55 g/1³/₄ oz.

Spread out over the baking sheet (they won't spread too much during cooking, but if your sheet isn't big enough you may need to cook them in batches). Bake for about 14 minutes, then cool on the sheet for 15 minutes. Transfer to a wire rack to cool completely before eating.

COOK'S TIP *Make sure you use a gluten-free baking powder and cocoa powder if cooking for people with allergies or intolerances.*

APPLE, CINNAMON & CHICKPEA CAKE

½ x 400-g/14-oz. can chickpeas/
    garbanzo beans, drained
    and rinsed
150 g/1 cup plus 2 tbsp
    self-raising/self-rising flour
1 tbsp ground cinnamon
½ tsp fine salt
125 g/½ cup/1⅛ sticks unsalted
    butter, softened, plus extra
    for greasing
125 g/⅔ cup minus 2 tsp
    light soft brown sugar
2 eggs
60 ml/4 tbsp full-fat/whole milk
2 apples, such as Royal Gala,
    peeled, cored and cut into
    1-cm/½-inch dice

TOPPING
50 g/generous ⅓ cup icing/
    confectioners' sugar
2 tsp full-fat/whole milk
a dash of vanilla bean paste
    (optional)

20-cm/8-inch square cake tin

SERVES 8

Preheat the oven to 180°C/160°C fan/350°F/Gas 4. Grease and line the cake tin with baking parchment.

In a bowl, crush the chickpeas with the back of a fork until well mashed. In another bowl, mix the flour, cinnamon and salt; set aside.

Using electric beaters, in a large mixing bowl cream together the butter and sugar for 2–3 minutes until light and fluffy. Beat in the eggs one at a time, then beat in the crushed chickpeas. Next, gently beat in the dry ingredients until just combined. Stir in the milk and half of the diced apple until combined.

Tip the mixture into the cake tin. Level the top and scatter over the remaining apple. Bake for about 45–50 minutes until golden, risen and a skewer inserted into the centre comes out clean. Set aside to cool in the tin.

For the topping, place the icing sugar, milk and vanilla (if using) in a bowl. Stir to a smooth, thick icing. You may need to add a splash more milk or a bit more icing sugar to get the right consistency. Drizzle over the cake, leave to set for 5 minutes, then slice to serve.

I used to make this cake with a light olive oil until prices sky-rocketed, so vegetable or sunflower oil will do. This is an elegant cake, perfect for afternoon tea and best served with a dollop of Greek yogurt.

ORANGE, POLENTA & WHITE BEAN CAKE

175 ml/³/₄ cup vegetable oil, plus extra for greasing

¹/₂ x 400-g/14-oz. can cannellini beans, drained and rinsed

3 eggs

175 g/scant 1 cup caster/superfine sugar

grated zest of 2 oranges

50 g/6 tbsp self-raising/self-rising flour

150 g/1¹/₂ cups ground almonds

100 g/²/₃ cup polenta/cornmeal

¹/₂ tsp baking powder

¹/₂ tsp salt

Greek yogurt and pomegranate seeds, to serve (optional)

CITRUS SYRUP

juice of 2 oranges

1 tbsp lemon juice

100 g/¹/₂ cup caster/superfine sugar

20-cm/8-inch loose-bottomed cake tin

SERVES 10

Preheat the oven to 180°C/160°C fan/350°F/Gas 4. Lightly grease the cake tin and line with baking parchment.

Whizz together the oil and beans in a blender until smooth.

In a large mixing bowl, use electric beaters to beat the eggs and sugar for 2–3 minutes until light and fluffy. Beat in the oil and bean mixture along with the orange zest. Add the flour, almonds, polenta, baking powder and salt and beat on a low speed until just combined. Tip into the tin and bake for 45–50 minutes until golden, risen and a skewer inserted into the centre of the cake comes out clean.

While the cake is in the oven make the syrup. Place the citrus juices and sugar in a small saucepan and warm until the sugar melts. Turn up the heat and simmer briskly for 2–3 minutes, then take off the heat and cool.

Allow the cake to cool for a couple of minutes when it comes out of the oven, then pierce all over with a skewer. Spoon the cooled syrup carefully all over the cake. Leave in the tin to cool. It can be served warm or at room temperature, ideally with a spoonful of Greek yogurt and some pomegranate seeds.

COOK'S TIP *You can make a gluten-free version of this cake by swapping the self-raising flour for a gluten-free version (and a gluten-free baking powder). Or you can swap the flour for the same quantity of ground almonds plus an extra ¹/₂ teaspoon baking powder; you may get slightly less rise but it will still taste fantastic.*

As an egg eater, I have never had a reason to make meringue from aquafaba, which is the name for the starchy, viscous liquid in a jar or can of chickpeas (or indeed any beans). Having cooked this a few times now I can say it works very well, makes a great egg-free pavlova and is a good use for an otherwise wasted by-product. A free-standing mixer is best here as you need to whisk the aquafaba for about 15 minutes (longer than a traditional egg meringue).

AQUAFABA MERINGUES

5 tbsp chickpea/garbanzo bean aquafaba
100 g/½ cup caster/ superfine sugar

FILLING
100 ml/scant ½ cup double/ heavy cream (or dairy-free alternative for vegans)
100 g/scant ½ cup Greek yogurt (or dairy-free alternative for vegans)
1 tsp vanilla extract
seasonal fruit, to serve

SERVES 4

Pop the aquafaba in the fridge for 30 minutes or in the freezer for 10 minutes.

Preheat the oven to 120°C/100°C fan/250°F/Gas ½. Line a large baking sheet with baking parchment.

Place the chilled aquafaba in the bowl of a free-standing mixer and whisk on a high speed for 5 minutes until stiff. With the whisk still running, add the sugar one spoonful at a time whisking well between each addition. Once all the sugar is incorporated continue whisking for about 5 minutes. Rub a little of the mixture between your fingers; it's ready when you can no longer feel any grains of sugar in the mix.

Spoon 4 meringue nests onto the lined baking sheet, spacing them well apart. Use a spoon to create a dip or crater in the centre. Bake for 2 hours. Turn off the oven, prop the door open with a tea/dish towel and allow the meringues to cool inside the oven for a further 2 hours.

To make the filling, whisk the cream, yogurt and vanilla together lightly to soft peaks. Spoon onto the meringues and top with seasonal fruit.

COOK'S TIP *Check the label on the canned or jarred chickpeas you use. Many options contain added salt and other preserving agents. Try to find ones that are just chickpeas and water for this recipe. I have had the best results with the aquafaba from a good quality jar of chickpeas, such as those from Bold Bean Co.*

INDEX

ACKNOWLEDGEMENTS

It has been an absolute pleasure to write this book, and I am so grateful to the many talented people who have worked so hard on it and helped to bring it to life. I am very aware that as an author a book may bear my name, yet there is a whole team without whom it would not have happened.

Firstly, a huge thanks to the whole team at Ryland Peters & Small, particularly to Julia Charles for giving me this wonderful opportunity and for making the process so seamless and enjoyable. To Abi Waters for pulling everything together so gracefully and for being so lovely to work with. To Toni Kay for your elegant design and crafty flower picking. And to Leslie Harrington, Megan Smith, Patricia Harrington and Yvonne Doolan.

Mowie Kay – your photography is beautiful, you have effortless style and you are such a calm and creative presence. Our shoot days were just lovely.

Troy Willis – you are such a talented food stylist. I could not have asked for someone who understood my recipes better or could make them look more beautiful.

Hannah Wilkinson – your props were just perfect and really made the food shine.

Jessica Geddes – you are a true pleasure to work with.

Arnaud Berrabia & Allegra D'Agostini – thank you for your hard work.

Mum – for reading everything I send you.

Tom – my chief taster, expert washer upper and my constant support. Thank you for everything.

Maya – you don't like pulses (yet!) but you make me happier than I could ever imagine. This book is for you.